Collins

PRACTICE MULTIPLE CHOICE QUESTIONS
CSEC®
Chemistry

Anne
Tindale

HarperCollins Publishers Ltd
The News Building
1 London Bridge Street
London SE1 9GF

First edition 2017

10 9 8 7 6 5 4 3

ISBN 978-0-00-819472-7

Collins® is a registered trademark of HarperCollins Publishers Limited.

Practice Multiple Choice Questions: CSEC® Chemistry is an independent publication and has not been authorised, sponsored or otherwise approved by **CXC®**.

CSEC® is a registered trademark of the **Caribbean Examinations Council (CXC®)**.

www.collins.co.uk/caribbeanschools

A catalogue record for this book is available from the British Library.

Typeset by QBS Learning
Printed and bound by CPI Group (UK) Ltd, Croydon CR0 4YY

Author: Anne Tindale
Publisher: Elaine Higgleton
Commissioning Editor: Ben Gardiner
Managing Editor: Sarah Thomas
Project Manager: Alissa McWhinnie
Copy Editor: Sophia Ktori
Proofreader: Angela Gardner
Answer Checker: Laura Quinlan
Artwork: QBS Learning
Cover design: Kevin Robbins and Gordon MacGilp
Production: Lauren Crisp

MIX
Paper from
responsible sources
FSC® C007454

FSC™ is a non-profit international organisation established to promote the responsible management of the world's forests. Products carrying the FSC label are independently certified to assure consumers that they come from forests that are managed to meet the social, economic and ecological needs of present and future generations, and other controlled sources.

Find out more about HarperCollins and the environment at
www.harpercollins.co.uk/green

Contents

Introduction iv

Section A: Principles of Chemistry 1

A1 States of Matter 1

A2 Mixtures and Separations 6

A3 Atomic Structure 12

A4 Periodic Table and Periodicity 17

A5 Structure and Bonding 22

A6 The Mole Concept (1) 27

A7 The Mole Concept (2) 31

A8 Acids, Bases and Salts (1) 34

A9 Acids, Bases and Salts (2) 37

A10 Oxidation-reduction Reactions 42

A11 Electrochemistry 46

A12 Rates of Reaction 53

A13 Energetics 57

Section B: Organic Chemistry 64

B1 Sources of Hydrocarbon Compounds 64

B2 Organic Chemistry – An Introduction 68

B3 Reactions of Carbon Compounds (1) 74

B4 Reactions of Carbon Compounds (2) 80

Section C: Inorganic Chemistry 87

C1 Characteristics of Metals 87

C2 Reactivity and Extraction of Metals 90

C3 Uses of Metals 96

C4 Impact of Metals on Living Systems and the Environment 98

C5 Non-metals (1) 101

C6 Non-metals (2) 105

C7 Qualitative Analysis 109

Download answers for free at www.collins.co.uk/caribbeanschools

Introduction

Structure of the CSEC® Chemistry Paper 1 Examination

There are **60 questions**, known as **items**, in the Paper 1 examination and the duration of the examination is **1 ¼ hours**. The paper is worth **30%** of your final examination mark.

Approximately half of the questions in the Paper 1 examination test topics in Section A, a quarter test topics in Section B and a quarter test topics in Section C.

Section	*Approximate* Number of Questions
A: Principles of Chemistry	30
B: Organic Chemistry	15
C: Inorganic Chemistry	15
Total	**60**

The questions test two profiles, **knowledge and comprehension**, and **use of knowledge**. Questions will be presented in a variety of ways including the use of diagrams, data, graphs, prose or other stimulus material.

Each question is allocated 1 mark. You will <u>not</u> lose a mark if a question is answered incorrectly.

Examination Tips
General strategies for answering multiple choice questions

- Read every word of each question very carefully and make sure you understand exactly what it is asking. Even if you think that the question appears simple or straightforward there may be important information you could easily omit, especially small, but very important words such as *all* or *only*.
- When faced with a question that seems unfamiliar, read it very carefully. Underline or circle the key pieces of information provided. Re-read the question if necessary to make sure that you are not misinterpreting the question and that you are very clear as to what is being asked.
- Each question has four options, **(A)**, **(B)**, **(C)** and **(D)**, and only one is the correct answer. Do not stop as soon as you come across an option that you think is the one required. Look at all the options very carefully as the differences between them may be very subtle. Cross out options that you know are incorrect for certain. There may be two options that appear very similar; identify the difference between the two so that you can select the correct answer.
- You have approximately 1 ¼ minutes per question. Some questions can be answered in less than 1 minute while other questions may require longer because of the reasoning or calculation involved. Do not spend too long on any one question.
- If a question appears difficult place a mark, such as an asterisk, on your answer sheet alongside the question number and return to it when you have finished answering all the other questions.
- Remember to carefully remove the asterisk, or other markings, from the answer sheet using a good clean eraser as soon as you have completed the question.
- Answer every question. Marks are not deducted for incorrect answers. Therefore, it is in your best interest to make an educated guess in instances where you do not know the answer. Never leave a question unanswered.
- Always ensure that you are shading the correct question number on your answer sheet. It is very easy to make a mistake, especially if you plan on returning to skipped questions.

- Some questions may ask which of the options is NOT correct or is INCORRECT, or they may state that all options are correct EXCEPT. Pay close attention to these questions because it is easy to fail to see these key words and answer the questions incorrectly.

- When answering a question that asks which option is NOT correct, is INCORRECT or that uses the word EXCEPT, place a T or an F next to each option to indicate if it is true or false. The correct answer to the question is the one with the *F*.

- Some questions may give two or more answers that could be correct and you are asked to determine which is the BEST or MOST LIKELY. You must consider each answer very carefully before making your choice because the differences between them may be very subtle.

- When a question gives three or four answers numbered **I**, **II** and **III** or **I**, **II**, **III** and **IV**, one or more of these answers may be correct. You will then be given four combinations as options, for example:

  A   I only

  B   I and II only

  C   II and III only

  D   I, II and III

  Place a tick by all the answers that you think are correct before you decide on the final correct combination.

- Do not make any assumptions about your choice of options. Just because two answers in succession have been **C**, it does not mean that the next one cannot be **C** as well.

- Try to leave time at the end of the examination to check over your answers, but never change an answer until you have thought about it again very carefully.

Strategies for the CSEC® Chemistry Paper 1

- Non-programmable calculators are allowed in the examination; however, when you use your calculator, always recheck your answer since it is easy to press the wrong key.

- If possible, when answering questions requiring you to perform a calculation, have a rough idea of what the answer should be. For example, if the mass of 1 mol of a substance is 40 g, then 16 g of the substance must be less than 1 mol; the answer must be 0.4 mol (16 ÷ 40) and not 2.5 mol (40 × 16) or 640 mol (40 × 16). Always work out the answer by writing your working on the question paper before you look at the options. If you do not find your answer in the options you can then go back and recheck your working for mistakes.

- If the question requires recall of a simple fact, such as the name of a piece of apparatus or a process, it is better to try to work out the answer before looking at the options given. Looking at the answers first could influence your choice and you may select an incorrect answer.

- When questions name chemical substances, read each name very carefully since some names are very similar, for example, *sulfide*, *sulfite* and *sulfate*.

- When questions involve equations, you must consider all the state symbols very carefully since the correct answer may depend on you recognising the correct states of the substances involved. For example, this question which asks what method would be used to separate the lead(II) iodide from the mixture in the following reaction:

$$Pb(NO_3)_2(aq) + 2KI(aq) \rightarrow PbI_2(s) + 2KNO_3(aq)$$

The state symbol for each reactant and potassium nitrate is (aq), and for lead(II) iodide it is (s). Lead(II) iodide would, therefore, be present as a precipitate in an aqueous solution so would be separated by filtration.

- The multiple choice examination focuses on detail. Make sure you learn all the facts, however small, that you have been taught.

Helpful Data

Relative atomic masses:

H = 1	Ne = 20	P = 31	Ca = 40
C = 12	Na = 23	S = 32	Fe = 56
N = 14	Mg = 24	Cl = 35.5	Cu = 64
O = 16	Al = 27	K = 39	Pb = 207

Avogadro's constant = 6.0×10^{23}

Molar volume at stp = 22.4 dm^3

Molar volume at rtp = 24.0 dm^3

Faraday constant = 96 500 C mol^{-1}

Section A: Principles of Chemistry
A1 States of Matter

1 Which of the following is NOT a feature that supports the particulate theory of matter?

(A) There are empty spaces between the particles.   (A)

(B) The particles are in constant motion.   (B)

(C) There are no forces of attraction between the particles.   (C)

(D) Temperature has an effect on the speed of motion of the particles.   (D)

<u>Items 2–3</u> refer to the following information.

A piece of apparatus was set up as illustrated below and a white ring quickly formed in the tube.

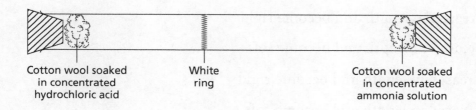

Cotton wool soaked in concentrated hydrochloric acid   White ring   Cotton wool soaked in concentrated ammonia solution

2 Which of the following equations correctly represents the reaction that formed the white ring?

(A) $NH_3(aq) + HCl(aq) \longrightarrow NH_4Cl(g)$ (A)

(B) $NH_3(g) + HCl(g) \longrightarrow NH_4Cl(g)$ (B)

(C) $NH_3(aq) + HCl(aq) \longrightarrow NH_4Cl(s)$ (C)

(D) $NH_3(g) + HCl(g) \longrightarrow NH_4Cl(s)$ (D)

3 The white ring formed in the position shown because

(A) ammonia molecules diffuse faster than hydrogen chloride molecules   (A)

(B) ammonia molecules are heavier than hydrogen chloride molecules   (B)

(C) hydrogen chloride molecules possess more kinetic energy than ammonia molecules   (C)

(D) hydrogen chloride molecules diffuse faster than ammonia molecules   (D)

4 Which of the following BEST describes what happens during osmosis?

  (A) Molecules move from a dilute solution to a more concentrated solution through a differentially permeable membrane.   Ⓐ

  (B) Water molecules diffuse from a dilute solution to a concentrated solution.   Ⓑ

  (C) Water molecules move through a differentially permeable membrane from a dilute solution to a concentrated solution.   Ⓒ

  (D) Water molecules diffuse from a concentrated solution to a dilute solution through a differentially permeable membrane.   Ⓓ

5 A strip of paw-paw is placed in a beaker of water. After 30 minutes it was found that the strip had

  (A) increased in length and become rigid   Ⓐ

  (B) increased in length and become soft   Ⓑ

  (C) decreased in length and become rigid   Ⓒ

  (D) decreased in length and become soft   Ⓓ

Item **6** refers to the piece of apparatus in the diagram below.

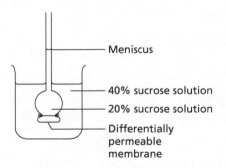

6 After 30 minutes the meniscus would have

  (A) moved up   Ⓐ

  (B) moved down   Ⓑ

  (C) remained in the same position   Ⓒ

  (D) moved up for a while and then moved down   Ⓓ

7 Sodium chloride can be used to preserve meat because

    I it draws water out of the cells of the meat by osmosis

    II it is toxic to bacteria and fungi

    III it inhibits the growth of microorganisms by causing water to enter their cells

(A) I only   Ⓐ

(B) II only   Ⓑ

(C) I and III only   Ⓒ

(D) I, II and III   Ⓓ

8 In a gas, the particles

(A) have small spaces between them   Ⓐ

(B) possess very little kinetic energy   Ⓑ

(C) vibrate in their fixed positions   Ⓒ

(D) are attracted to each other by weak forces   Ⓓ

9 Compared to the particles in liquids, the particles in solids

(A) have more space between them   Ⓐ

(B) have less kinetic energy   Ⓑ

(C) move faster   Ⓒ

(D) have weaker forces of attraction between them   Ⓒ

Items **10–11** refer to the table below, which gives the melting and boiling points of four substances. In answering the items, each option may be used once, more than once or not at all.

Substance	Melting point/°C	Boiling point/°C
I	86	211
II	−173	−10
III	−65	97
IV	309	762

10 Which substance will be a gas at room temperature?

(A) I   (A)

(B) II   (B)

(C) III   (C)

(D) IV   (D)

11 Which substance will be composed of slow moving particles at room temperature?

(A) I   (A)

(B) II   (B)

(C) III   (C)

(D) IV   (D)

12 Changing a solid to a liquid is known as

(A) melting   (A)

(B) dissolving   (B)

(C) freezing   (C)

(D) evaporating   (D)

13 Which of the following prolonged operations CANNOT result in either boiling or freezing?

(A) Cooling nitrogen gas   Ⓐ

(B) Heating liquid sodium chloride   Ⓑ

(C) Cooling ethanol   Ⓒ

(D) Heating iodine crystals   Ⓓ

14 Evaporation ONLY occurs

(A) during boiling   Ⓐ

(B) at a specific temperature   Ⓑ

(C) when heat is applied to a liquid   Ⓒ

(D) at the surface of a liquid   Ⓓ

15 Which of the following BEST describes what happens to particles as a liquid freezes?

(A) They gain kinetic energy and lose freedom of movement.   Ⓐ

(B) They lose kinetic energy and lose freedom of movement.   Ⓑ

(C) They lose kinetic energy and become more spread out.   Ⓒ

(D) They gain kinetic energy and become more ordered.   Ⓓ

16 Which of the following substances sublime when heated?

    I Carbon monoxide

    II Carbon dioxide

    III Naphthalene

(A) I and II only   Ⓐ

(B) I and III only   Ⓑ

(C) II and III only   Ⓒ

(D) I, II and III   Ⓓ

Items **17–18** refer to the graph below, which shows the heating curve for substance X.

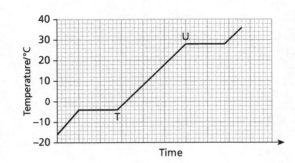

17 The freezing point of substance X is

(A) –16 °C   Ⓐ

(B) –6 °C   Ⓑ

(C) –4 °C   Ⓒ

(D) 28 °C   Ⓓ

18 The particles between T and U are

(A) gaining kinetic energy and moving faster   Ⓐ

(B) gaining kinetic energy and moving closer together   Ⓑ

(C) losing kinetic energy and moving more slowly   Ⓒ

(D) losing kinetic energy and moving further apart   Ⓓ

A2 Mixtures and Separations

1 Which of the following statements is true?

(A) The composition of a pure substance is variable.   Ⓐ

(B) The density of a pure substance is fixed.   Ⓑ

(C) The component parts of a mixture cannot be separated by any means.   Ⓒ

(D) The properties of mixtures are fixed and constant.   Ⓓ

2 The presence of a small amount of sodium chloride in water is MOST likely to

(A) increase the water's boiling point and decrease the water's melting point ⒶA

(B) increase the water's boiling point and increase the water's freezing point ⒷB

(C) decrease the water's boiling point and decrease the water's melting point ⒸC

(D) have no effect on the water's boiling point and decrease the water's freezing point ⒹD

3 An alloy may be classified as

(A) a solution ⒶA

(B) a colloid ⒷB

(C) a suspension ⒸC

(D) a pure substance ⒹD

4 Which of the following lists consists ONLY of colloids?

(A) Mayonnaise, smoke, air, gelatin ⒶA

(B) Sea water, milk, fog, smoke ⒷB

(C) Milk, shaving cream, white vinegar, air ⒸC

(D) Mayonnaise, fog, smoke, shaving cream ⒹD

5 Which of the following statements is true?

(A) The dispersed particles in a colloid are larger than those in a suspension. ⒶA

(B) Solutions are usually opaque. ⒷB

(C) If left undisturbed, the dispersed particles in a suspension will not settle. ⒸC

(D) Light does not pass through a suspension. ⒹD

Items **6–8** refer to the following graph, which shows how the solubilities of four salts vary with temperature.

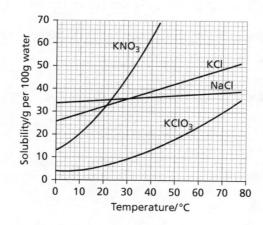

6 Which salt is the LEAST soluble at 35 °C?

(A) NaCl Ⓐ

(B) KCl Ⓑ

(C) $KClO_3$ Ⓒ

(D) KNO_3 Ⓓ

7 Temperature change has the GREATEST effect on the solubility of

(A) NaCl Ⓐ

(B) KCl Ⓑ

(C) $KClO_3$ Ⓒ

(D) KNO_3 Ⓓ

8 A solution of $KClO_3$ is saturated at 64 °C. If this solution is cooled to 12 °C, what mass of crystals would form?

(A) 31 g Ⓐ

(B) 26 g Ⓑ

(C) 21 g Ⓒ

(D) 5 g Ⓓ

9 Two liquids, Y and Z, were placed in a separating funnel and two layers formed as in the diagram below.

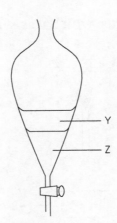

From this it can be deduced that liquid Y

    I is oil

    II has a lower density than liquid Z

    III has a lower boiling point than liquid Z

    IV is immiscible with liquid Z

(A) I and II only   Ⓐ

(B) II and IV only   Ⓑ

(C) I, II and IV only   Ⓒ

(D) II, III and IV only   Ⓓ

10 A forensic scientist wishes to separate the dyes in a sample of black ink found at a crime scene. What technique would she use?

(A) Simple distillation   Ⓐ

(B) Chromatography   Ⓑ

(C) Crystallisation   Ⓒ

(D) Fractional distillation   Ⓓ

<u>Item 11</u> refers to the following apparatus, which was set up to separate sand from sea water.

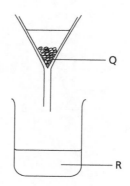

11 Which of the following correctly identifies Q and R?

	Q	R	
(A)	Residue	Filtrate	Ⓐ
(B)	Residue	Distillate	Ⓑ
(C)	Filtrate	Residue	Ⓒ
(D)	Distillate	Residue	Ⓓ

12 A mixture of ethanol and water can be separated based on their different

(A) boiling points   Ⓐ

(B) melting points   Ⓑ

(C) densities   Ⓒ

(D) solubilities   Ⓓ

13 Which of the following arrangements would be the MOST suitable to obtain pure water from sea water?

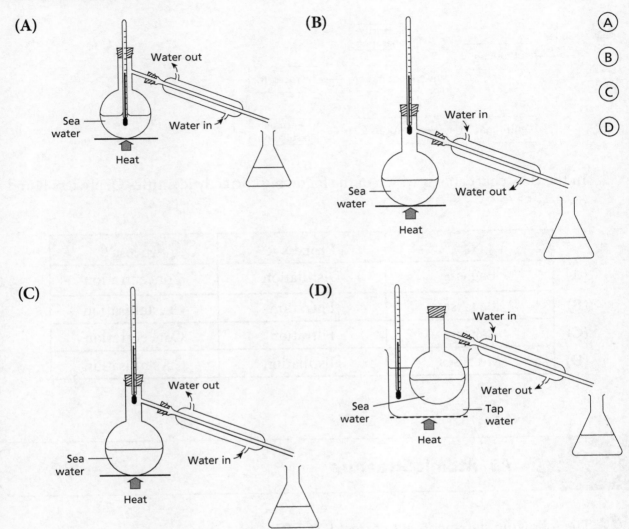

(A)

(B)

(C)

(D)

Ⓐ

Ⓑ

Ⓒ

Ⓓ

14 During the extraction of sucrose from sugar cane, lime (calcium hydroxide) is added to the dilute cane juice to

    I make the juice more acidic

    II stop the sucrose breaking down into glucose and fructose

    III precipitate out impurities

(A) I only

(B) III only

(C) II and III only

(D) I, II and III

Ⓐ

Ⓑ

Ⓒ

Ⓓ

15

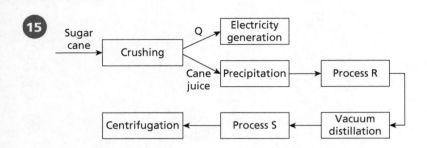

In the flow chart above, which of the following correctly identifies Q, process R and process S?

	Q	Process R	Process S
(A)	Bagasse	Distillation	Concentration
(B)	Bagasse	Filtration	Crystallisation
(C)	Bagasse	Filtration	Concentration
(D)	Molasses	Distillation	Crystallisation

A ⃝ B ⃝ C ⃝ D ⃝

A3 Atomic Structure

1 The following statements are correct EXCEPT

(A) An atom is the smallest unit of an element that can exist by itself Ⓐ

(B) Electrons orbiting around the nucleus of an atom make up most of the mass of the atom Ⓑ

(C) An atom has no overall charge Ⓒ

(D) Electrons orbiting the nucleus of an atom do so in energy shells Ⓓ

2 Which of the following is correct?

(A) An electron and a neutron are the same size.

(B) The total number of protons in an atom of an element is different from the total number of electrons.

(C) The mass of a proton is $\frac{1}{1840}$ the mass of an electron.

(D) The mass of a proton is equal to the mass of a neutron.

(A)

(B)

(C)

(D)

3 Which of the following correctly summarises the relative charges on the three subatomic particles?

	Relative charge		
	Proton	**Neutron**	**Electron**
(A)	+1	−1	0
(B)	0	−1	+1
(C)	−1	+1	0
(D)	+1	0	−1

(A)

(B)

(C)

(D)

4 Which of the following gives the number of subatomic particles in an atom of chromium, $^{52}_{24}\text{Cr}$?

	Number of:		
	Protons	**Neutrons**	**Electrons**
(A)	24	24	28
(B)	24	28	24
(C)	24	52	24
(D)	28	24	28

(A)

(B)

(C)

(D)

5 The mass number of an element whose atoms contain 15 protons, 16 neutrons and 15 electrons is

(A) 32   Ⓐ

(B) 31   Ⓑ

(C) 16   Ⓒ

(D) 15   Ⓓ

6 The nuclear notation of a silver atom is $^{108}_{47}\text{Ag}$. This means that

    I an atom of silver has 47 neutrons

    II the mass number of silver is 108

    III an atom of silver has 47 electrons

    IV the atomic number of silver is 61

(A) I and II only   Ⓐ

(B) I and IV only   Ⓑ

(C) II and III only   Ⓒ

(D) II, III and IV only   Ⓓ

7 The mass number of copper is 64. If a copper atom has 35 neutrons, the atomic number of copper is

(A) 29   Ⓐ

(B) 35   Ⓑ

(C) 64   Ⓒ

(D) 70   Ⓓ

8 The electronic configuration of an atom of fluorine, $^{19}_{9}\text{F}$, is

(A) 2,7   Ⓐ

(B) 2,8   Ⓑ

(C) 2,8,1   Ⓒ

(D) 2,8,8,1   Ⓓ

9 Which of the following is the MOST accurately drawn shell diagram of an atom that has an atomic number of 6 and a mass number of 13?

(A)

(B)

(C)

(D)

Ⓐ

Ⓑ

Ⓒ

Ⓓ

Item **10** refers to the following shell diagram showing an atom of element Z.

10 Given that element Z has 12 neutrons in its nucleus, which of the following is NOT true about element Z?

(A) Z has a mass number of 23.

(B) An atom of Z has 11 protons in its nucleus.

(C) The chemical properties of Z are very similar to those of aluminium, $_{13}^{27}Al$.

(D) An atom of Z has 1 valence electron.

Ⓐ

Ⓑ

Ⓒ

Ⓓ

11 The chemical properties of an element are determined mainly by

    I the arrangement of electrons in its atoms

    II the number of protons in the nuclei of its atoms

    III its mass number

(A) I only

(B) II only

(C) II and III only

(D) I, II and III

Ⓐ

Ⓑ

Ⓒ

Ⓓ

12 Isotopes have the same

(A) physical properties　　　　　　　　　　　　　　　　　　　　Ⓐ

(B) chemical properties　　　　　　　　　　　　　　　　　　　　Ⓑ

(C) number of neutrons　　　　　　　　　　　　　　　　　　　　Ⓒ

(D) mass number　　　　　　　　　　　　　　　　　　　　　　Ⓓ

13 Which of the following pairs represents isotopes of element R?

(A) ^y_xR　　　and　　　$^{y+2}_{x+2}R$　　　　　　　　　　　　　Ⓐ

(B) ^y_xR　　　and　　　$^{y+2}_{2x}R$　　　　　　　　　　　　　Ⓑ

(C) ^y_xR　　　and　　　$^{y+2}_xR$　　　　　　　　　　　　　Ⓒ

(D) ^y_xR　　　and　　　$^y_{x+2}R$　　　　　　　　　　　　　Ⓓ

14 Naturally occurring element T consists of 90% $^{24}_{12}T$ and 10% $^{25}_{12}T$. The average mass number of element T is

(A) 24.1　　　　　　　　　　　　　　　　　　　　　　　　　Ⓐ

(B) 24.2　　　　　　　　　　　　　　　　　　　　　　　　　Ⓑ

(C) 24.5　　　　　　　　　　　　　　　　　　　　　　　　　Ⓒ

(D) 24.9　　　　　　　　　　　　　　　　　　　　　　　　　Ⓓ

15 Which of the following is NOT a use of radioactive isotopes?

(A) Radiotherapy　　　　　　　　　　　　　　　　　　　　　Ⓐ

(B) Generating electricity　　　　　　　　　　　　　　　　　　Ⓑ

(C) As tracers in medical examinations　　　　　　　　　　　　　Ⓒ

(D) Dating dinosaur remains　　　　　　　　　　　　　　　　　Ⓓ

16 Chlorine's relative atomic mass is 35.5. The half (0.5) is due to

(A) half a proton   Ⓐ

(B) half a neutron   Ⓑ

(C) half an electron   Ⓒ

(D) the existence of isotopes   Ⓓ

A4 Periodic Table and Periodicity

<u>Items **1–2**</u> refer to the following options.

(A) Henry Moseley

(B) Dmitri Mendeleev

(C) John Newlands

(D) Johann Döbereiner

Match EACH item below with one of the options above. Each option may be used once, more than once or not at all.

1 He proposed the Law of Octaves.

(A)   Ⓐ

(B)   Ⓑ

(C)   Ⓒ

(D)   Ⓓ

2 He is widely credited with creating the first version of the periodic table.

(A)   Ⓐ

(B)   Ⓑ

(C)   Ⓒ

(D)   Ⓓ

3 Elements in the modern periodic table are arranged on the basis of

     I their increasing relative atomic mass

    II their chemical properties

   III the electronic configuration of their atoms

(A) I only   Ⓐ

(B) I and III only   Ⓑ

(C) II and III only   Ⓒ

(D) I, II and III   Ⓓ

4 Elements in Group II of the periodic table are known as

(A) noble gases   Ⓐ

(B) alkali metals   Ⓑ

(C) alkaline metals   Ⓒ

(D) alkaline earth metals Ⓓ

5 The following statements about the periodic table are correct EXCEPT

(A) Moving down a group the metallic nature of elements decreases   Ⓐ

(B) Moving along a period from left to right the non-metallic nature of elements increases   Ⓑ

(C) All elements in the same period have the same number of occupied electron shells   Ⓒ

(D) All elements in the same group have the same number of valence electrons   Ⓓ

6 Elements in Group 0 of the periodic table

(A) have 8 electrons in their valence electron shells   Ⓐ

(B) are very reactive   Ⓑ

(C) have full valence electron shells.   Ⓒ

(D) are solids at room temperature.   Ⓓ

7 Element R is in Group IV and Period 5 of the periodic table. An atom of R would be expected to have

(A) 5 occupied electron shells and 4 valence electrons ⒜

(B) 4 occupied electron shells and 5 valence electrons Ⓑ

(C) 5 occupied electron shells and 6 valence electrons Ⓒ

(D) 6 occupied electron shells and 5 valence electrons Ⓓ

8 An element with an atomic number of 7 would be expected to

(A) be in Period 1 of the periodic table ⒜

(B) be a non-metal Ⓑ

(C) be in Group VII of the periodic table Ⓒ

(D) have a stable electronic structure Ⓓ

9 Which set of three elements, identified by their atomic numbers, all belong to the same period of the periodic table?

	Atomic number		
	Element I	**Element II**	**Element III**
(A)	3	11	19	⒜
(B)	4	13	18	Ⓑ
(C)	11	14	17	Ⓒ
(D)	12	16	20	Ⓓ

10 The electronic configuration of an atom of element Z is 2,8,8,2. Element Z would be expected to

  I be in Group II of the periodic table

  II be more reactive than $_{12}^{24}Mg$

  III react with hydrochloric acid

(A) I only ⒜

(B) II only Ⓑ

(C) I and III only Ⓒ

(D) I, II and III Ⓓ

11 The chemical properties of calcium are MOST similar to those of

(A) aluminium   Ⓐ

(B) barium   Ⓑ

(C) potassium   Ⓒ

(D) strontium   Ⓓ

12 Which element has the GREATEST strength of oxidising power?

(A) Fluorine   Ⓐ

(B) Chlorine   Ⓑ

(C) Bromine   Ⓒ

(D) Iodine   Ⓓ

13

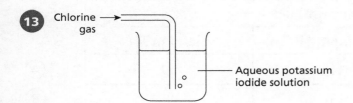

Chlorine gas →

Aqueous potassium iodide solution

What colour change would be observed in the solution during the experiment illustrated above?

(A) Brown to colourless   Ⓐ

(B) Brown to green   Ⓑ

(C) Colourless to green   Ⓒ

(D) Colourless to brown   Ⓓ

14 Which of the following is NOT a correct statement?

(A) The electronic configuration of X is 2,8,7.

(B) X and Y are both halogens.

(C) X is more reactive than Y.

(D) Y is capable of displacing X from a solution containing the sodium salt of X.

15 Which of the following statements about X and Z is correct?

(A) Atom X has a larger atomic radius than atom Z.

(B) X ionises more readily than Z.

(C) X is a non-metal and Z is a metal.

(D) X is less reactive than Z.

16 Element R is found in Group I, Period 3 of the periodic table and element T is found in Group II, Period 3. It would be expected that

(A) R is more reactive than T

(B) the atoms of both elements have 3 valence electrons

(C) T ionises more readily than R

(D) both elements ionise by gaining electrons

1 Ionic bonding occurs between

(A) two metals. Ⓐ

(B) a metal and a non-metal Ⓑ

(C) a semi-metal and a non-metal Ⓒ

(D) two non-metals Ⓓ

2 The table below gives information about two particles. Some information has been omitted.

Particle	Atomic number	Number of electrons
^{56}Fe atom	26	
$^{56}Fe^{3+}$ ion		W

The number represented by W is

(A) 23 Ⓐ

(B) 26 Ⓑ

(C) 29 Ⓒ

(D) 30 Ⓓ

3 Fluorine has an atomic number of 9. Which of the following represents the electron arrangement in a fluoride ion?

(A)   (B)

Ⓐ

Ⓑ

Ⓒ

(C)   (D)

Ⓓ

4 Two atoms with atomic numbers 12 and 17 would

    (A) bond to form an ionic compound   Ⓐ

    (B) bond to form a covalent compound   Ⓑ

    (C) bond to form a metallic lattice   Ⓒ

    (D) not bond with each other   Ⓓ

<u>Item 5</u> refers to the following diagram of two atoms, R and T.

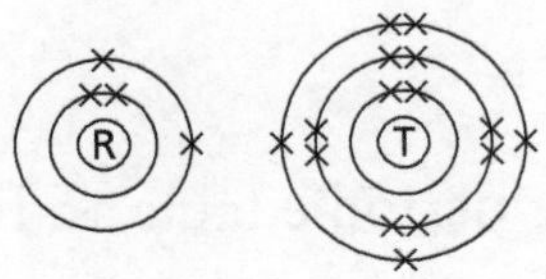

5 R and T form a compound with the formula

    (A) RT_2 Ⓐ

    (B) R_3T Ⓑ

    (C) R_2T_3 Ⓒ

    (D) R_3T_2 Ⓓ

6 A covalent compound is formed by

    (A) metal atoms losing valence electrons to non-metal atoms   Ⓐ

    (B) non-metal atoms losing valence electrons to metal atoms   Ⓑ

    (C) metal atoms sharing valence electrons   Ⓒ

    (D) non-metal atoms sharing valence electrons   Ⓓ

7 Oxygen atoms, $^{16}_{8}O$, bond covalently in pairs to form oxygen molecules. Which of the following MOST accurately represents an oxygen molecule?

    (A)   (B)   Ⓐ

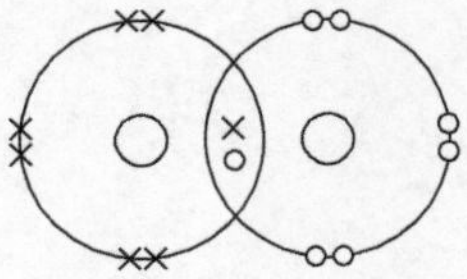

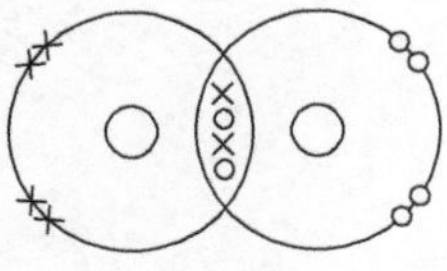

     Ⓑ

     Ⓒ

    (C) 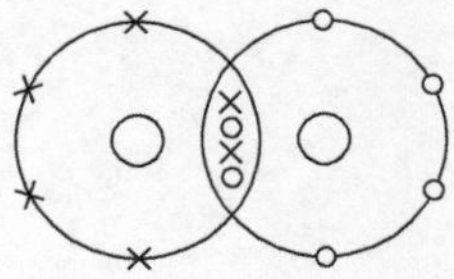   (D)   Ⓓ

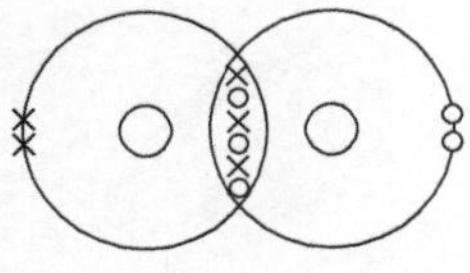

8 Particle Q has 16 protons, 17 neutrons and 18 electrons. Particle Q is

(A) an atom of a metal

Ⓐ

(B) an atom of a noble gas

Ⓑ

(C) an anion

Ⓒ

(D) a cation

Ⓓ

9 Element D is in Group III of the periodic table and element E is in Group VII. Which of the following represents the formula of the compound formed between D and E?

(A) DE_3

Ⓐ

(B) D_3E

Ⓑ

(C) D_7E_3

Ⓒ

(D) D_3E_7

Ⓓ

10 The following lists consist of ionic compounds EXCEPT

(A) barium hydroxide, zinc carbonate, ammonium sulfate

Ⓐ

(B) calcium chloride, carbon disulfide, magnesium nitrate

Ⓑ

(C) sodium sulfate, copper(II) oxide, potassium nitride

Ⓒ

(D) aluminium sulfide, sodium sulfite, calcium fluoride

Ⓓ

Items **11–12** refer to the four atoms illustrated below.

I

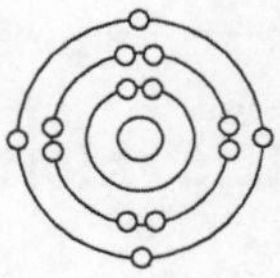

II

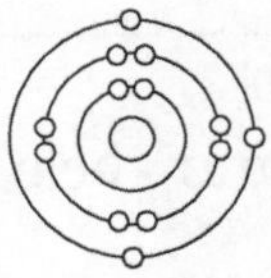

III

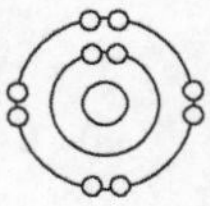

IV

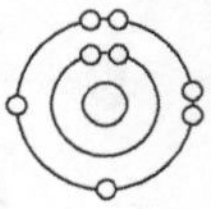

11 Which two atoms can combine to form a covalent compound?

(A) I and III   Ⓐ

(B) I and IV   Ⓑ

(C) II and III   Ⓒ

(D) II and IV   Ⓓ

12 Which atoms would form ions with the same electronic configuration?

(A) I and III   Ⓐ

(B) I and IV   Ⓑ

(C) II and III   Ⓒ

(D) II and IV   Ⓓ

13 Positive cations in a sea of delocalised electrons are found in

(A) ionic compounds   Ⓐ

(B) covalent compounds   Ⓑ

(C) aqueous solutions of ionic compounds   Ⓒ

(D) metals   Ⓓ

14 Simple molecular solids usually have low melting points because

(A) the intermolecular forces between the atoms are weak   Ⓐ

(B) the covalent bonds between the atoms are weak   Ⓑ

(C) the intermolecular forces between the molecules are weak   Ⓒ

(D) the forces between delocalised electrons and the molecules are weak   Ⓓ

25

Item 15 refers to the diagram below, which shows a portion of the sodium chloride lattice.

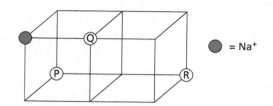

= Na⁺

15 Which combination gives the correct identities of P, Q and R?

	P	Q	R
(A)	Na^+	Cl^-	Cl^-
(B)	Na^+	Cl^-	Na^+
(C)	Cl^-	Cl^-	Na^+
(D)	Cl^-	Na^+	Cl^-

Ⓐ
Ⓑ
Ⓒ
Ⓓ

16 Which of the following is/are properties of ionic solids?

   I Most dissolve in water

   II They have high melting points

   III They do not conduct electricity at room temperature

(A) I only

(B) I and II only

(C) II and III only

(D) I, II and III

Ⓐ
Ⓑ
Ⓒ
Ⓓ

17 The lubricating properties of graphite can BEST be explained by the weak bonds

(A) between the layers of carbon atoms

(B) created by delocalised electrons

(C) between ions in the structure

(D) between carbon atoms within the layers

Ⓐ
Ⓑ
Ⓒ
Ⓓ

18 Diamond and graphite are allotropes of carbon because

(A) their atoms contain different numbers of neutrons (A)

(B) they have the same physical properties but different chemical properties (B)

(C) they exist in different physical states (C)

(D) in the same state, they have distinct physical structures (D)

19 When sodium chloride dissolves in water, the solution conducts electricity because

(A) electrons become delocalised and free to move (A)

(B) Na^+ and Cl^- ions become free to move (B)

(C) polar water molecules move and carry electricity (C)

(D) protons become free to move (D)

20 Which of the following is an element and forms crystals composed of small molecules?

(A) Water (A)

(B) Carbon dioxide (B)

(C) Iodine (C)

(D) Diamond (D)

A6 The Mole Concept (1)

1 Relative atomic mass compares the masses of atoms to

(A) the mass of a carbon-12 atom (A)

(B) the mass of a hydrogen atom (B)

(C) the mass of a proton (C)

(D) the mass of an electron (D)

Item 2 refers to the atoms illustrated below.

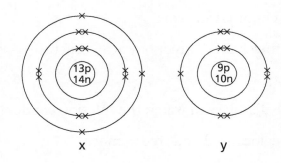

2 The atoms combine together to form a compound with a relative formula mass of

(A) 100   Ⓐ

(B) 84   Ⓑ

(C) 46   Ⓒ

(D) 40   Ⓓ

3 The molar mass of ammonium phosphate is

(A) 133 g mol^{-1} Ⓐ

(B) 144 g mol^{-1} Ⓑ

(C) 146 g mol^{-1} Ⓒ

(D) 149 g mol^{-1} Ⓓ

4 How many moles are there in 31.8 g of sodium carbonate?

(A) 0.03 mol   Ⓐ

(B) 0.3 mol   Ⓑ

(C) 0.333 mol   Ⓒ

(D) 3.333 mol   Ⓓ

5 Avogadro's constant is the same as the number of

      I magnesium atoms in 24 g of magnesium

      II nitrogen molecules in 14 g of nitrogen

      III copper(II) sulfate formula units in 160 g of copper(II) sulfate

(A) II only   Ⓐ

(B) I and III only   Ⓑ

(C) II and III only   Ⓒ

(D) I, II and III   Ⓓ

6 0.04 mol of aluminium oxide contains

(A) 2.4×10^{23} aluminium oxide formula units   Ⓐ

(B) 2.4×10^{24} aluminium oxide formula units   Ⓑ

(C) 4.8×10^{22} aluminium ions   Ⓒ

(D) 7.2×10^{23} oxide ions   Ⓓ

7 The following contain the same number of atoms as 12 g of carbon-12 EXCEPT

(A) 1 g of hydrogen   Ⓐ

(B) 56 g of iron   Ⓑ

(C) 17 g of ammonia   Ⓒ

(D) 20 g of neon   Ⓓ

8 The volume occupied by 0.25 mol of sulfur dioxide at rtp is

(A) $60 \, cm^3$ Ⓐ

(B) $600 \, cm^3$ Ⓑ

(C) $0.6 \, dm^3$ Ⓒ

(D) $6.0 \, dm^3$ Ⓓ

9 A gas jar that has a volume of 336 cm^3 is full of oxygen at stp. What mass of oxygen does it contain?

(A) 480 g   (A)

(B) 240 g   (B)

(C) 0.48 g   (C)

(D) 0.24 g   (D)

10 3.3 g of carbon dioxide

(A) contains the same number of molecules as 2.1 g of nitrogen   (A)

(B) has the same volume as 3.3 g of sulfur dioxide at stp   (B)

(C) contains 4.5×10^{23} carbon dioxide molecules   (C)

(D) is equivalent to 0.75 mol of carbon dioxide   (D)

11 A sample of hydrated iron(II) sulfate was found to be composed of 15.2 g of iron(II) sulfate and 12.6 g of water. If the relative formula mass of iron(II) sulfate is 152, then the formula of hydrated iron(II) sulfate is

(A) $FeSO_4.7H_2O$ (A)

(B) $FeSO_4.5H_2O$ (B)

(C) $FeSO_4.3H_2O$ (C)

(D) $FeSO_4.H_2O$ (D)

12 On analysis a compound was found to contain 41.55 g of element W and 8.45 g of element Z. If the relative atomic mass of W is 23 and of Z is 14, the empirical formula of the compound is

(A) WZ   (A)

(B) W_2Z (B)

(C) W_3Z (C)

(D) WZ_3 (D)

13 The GREATEST proportion by mass of nitrogen is present in

(A) NH_4NO_3 Ⓐ

(B) $(NH_4)_2SO_4$ Ⓑ

(C) $(NH_4)_3PO_4$ Ⓒ

(D) $Al(NO_3)_3$ Ⓓ

A7 The Mole Concept (2)

1 The Law of Conservation of Matter states that during a chemical reaction

(A) matter can be both created and destroyed   Ⓐ

(B) matter can be created but not destroyed   Ⓑ

(C) matter can be destroyed but not created   Ⓒ

(D) matter cannot be created or destroyed   Ⓓ

2 What are the correct coefficients needed to balance the following equation?

$$Al(s) + O_2(g) \longrightarrow Al_2O_3(s)$$

(A) 4, 3, 2   Ⓐ

(B) 2, 3, 4   Ⓑ

(C) 2, 3, 2   Ⓒ

(D) 4, 2, 3   Ⓓ

3 The following equation summarises the reaction occurring when copper(II) nitrate solution is added to sodium hydroxide solution.

$$Cu(NO_3)_2(aq) + 2NaOH(aq) \longrightarrow Cu(OH)_2(s) + 2NaNO_3(aq)$$

The correct ionic equation for the reaction is

(A) $2NO_3^-(aq) + 2Na^+(aq) \longrightarrow 2NaNO_3(aq)$ Ⓐ

(B) $Cu^{2+}(aq) + 2OH^-(aq) \longrightarrow Cu(OH)_2(s)$ Ⓑ

(C) $Cu(NO_3)_2(aq) + 2OH^-(aq) \longrightarrow Cu(OH)_2(s) + 2NO_3^-(aq)$ Ⓒ

(D) $Cu^{2+}(aq) + 2NaOH(aq) \longrightarrow Cu(OH)_2(s) + 2Na^+(aq)$ Ⓓ

4 Reacting a solution containing 23.4 g of sodium chloride with one containing excess lead(II) nitrate, according to the equation below, would produce what mass of lead(II) chloride?

$$Pb(NO_3)_2(aq) + 2NaCl(aq) \longrightarrow PbCl_2(s) + 2NaNO_3(aq)$$

(A) 11.7 g

(B) 23.4 g

(C) 55.6 g

(D) 111.2 g

Ⓐ

Ⓑ

Ⓒ

Ⓓ

5 What volume of ammonia, measured at rtp, could be produced by reacting 4.2 g of calcium oxide with excess ammonium sulfate according to the following equation?

$$CaO(s) + (NH_4)_2SO_4(s) \longrightarrow CaSO_4(s) + 2NH_3(g) + H_2O(l)$$

(A) 16.8 dm^3

(B) 14.4 dm^3

(C) 7.2 dm^3

(D) 3.6 dm^3

Ⓐ

Ⓑ

Ⓒ

Ⓓ

6 What volume of hydrogen, measured at stp, would be evolved when a solution of hydrochloric acid containing 0.05 g H$^+$ ions reacts with excess magnesium according to the following equation?

$$Mg(s) + 2H^+(aq) \longrightarrow Mg^{2+}(aq) + H_2(g)$$

(A) 2240 cm^3

(B) 1120 cm^3

(C) 560 cm^3

(D) 280 cm^3

Ⓐ

Ⓑ

Ⓒ

Ⓓ

7 A standard solution:

    I is saturated.

    II is made in a volumetric flask.

    III has a known concentration.

(A) I only   (A)

(B) I and II only   (B)

(C) II and III only   (C)

(D) I, II and III   (D)

8 The mass concentration of a solution of magnesium chloride containing 0.1 mol magnesium chloride in 250 cm^3 of solution is

(A) 2.375 g dm^{-3} (A)

(B) 9.5 g dm^{-3} (B)

(C) 19.0 g dm^{-3} (C)

(D) 38.0 g dm^{-3} (D)

9 What mass of sodium hydroxide is required to make 200 cm^3 of sodium hydroxide solution of concentration 0.4 mol dm^{-3}?

(A) 0.4 g   (A)

(B) 3.2 g   (B)

(C) 8.0 g   (C)

(D) 16.0 g   (D)

10 The reaction between aluminium hydroxide and hydrochloric acid is given in the equation below.

$$Al(OH)_3(s) + 3HCl(aq) \longrightarrow AlCl_3(aq) + 3H_2O(l)$$

50 cm^3 of hydrochloric acid of concentration 0.6 mol dm^{-3} reacts with excess aluminium hydroxide to form what mass of aluminium chloride?

(A) 1.335 g   (A)

(B) 4.005 g   (B)

(C) 26.7 g   (C)

(D) 80.1 g   (D)

A8 Acids, Bases and Salts (1)

1 Which of the following BEST explains why an acid is a proton donor?

(A) It contains H^+ ions   (A)

(B) Its molecules contain protons   (B)

(C) It gives H^+ ions to the other reactant when it reacts   (C)

(D) Its H^+ ions are protons   (D)

2 Which of the following is/are properties of aqueous acids?

    I They have a pH greater than 7

    II They turn red litmus paper blue

    III They conduct electricity

(A) I only   (A)

(B) III only   (B)

(C) II and III only   (C)

(D) I, II and III   (D)

3 Ethanoic acid is a weak acid because

(A) it is fully ionised in aqueous solution   (A)

(B) it is very dilute   (B)

(C) it does not ionise when placed in water   (C)

(D) its aqueous solution contains both acid molecules and H^+ ions   (D)

4 The MOST likely pH of aqueous hydrochloric acid is

(A) 1   (A)

(B) 5   (B)

(C) 8   (C)

(D) 13   (D)

5 Which of the following is a monobasic acid?

(A) H_2SO_3

(B) H_2SO_4

(C) H_2CO_2

(D) H_2CO_3

Ⓐ
Ⓑ
Ⓒ
Ⓓ

6 A student saw effervescence when he tried to clean some zinc-coated iron nails by placing them in dilute sulfuric acid. What gas was formed?

(A) Oxygen

(B) Carbon dioxide

(C) Water vapour

(D) Hydrogen

Ⓐ
Ⓑ
Ⓒ
Ⓓ

7 Hydrochloric acid reacts with all of the following EXCEPT

(A) sodium sulfate

(B) zinc oxide

(C) magnesium carbonate

(D) calcium hydroxide

Ⓐ
Ⓑ
Ⓒ
Ⓓ

8 Which equation shows the actual chemical change occurring when sodium carbonate reacts with hydrochloric acid?

(A) $CO_3^{2-}(aq) + H^+(aq) \longrightarrow CO_2(g) + H_2O(l)$

(B) $CO_3^{2-}(aq) + 2H^+(aq) \longrightarrow CO_2(g) + H_2O(l)$

(C) $Na^+(aq) + Cl^-(aq) \longrightarrow NaCl(aq)$

(D) $Na_2CO_3(aq) + 2HCl(aq) \longrightarrow NaCl(aq) + CO_2(g) + H_2O(l)$

Ⓐ
Ⓑ
Ⓒ
Ⓓ

9 Which of the following is INCORRECT?

(A) Methanoic acid is found in ant stings.

(B) Ethanoic acid is found in limes.

(C) Ascorbic acid is destroyed by heating.

(D) Lactic acid is produced in muscles during strenuous activity.

Ⓐ
Ⓑ
Ⓒ
Ⓓ

10 Aqueous alkalis

    I react with ammonium salts

    II neutralise acids

    III contain O^{2-} ions

  (A) I and II only   Ⓐ

  (B) I and III only   Ⓑ

  (C) II and III only   Ⓒ

  (D) I, II and III   Ⓓ

<u>Item 11</u> refers to the diagram below, which shows the pH scale and the colour of universal indicator.

0	1	2	3	4	5	6	7	8	9	10	11	12	13	14
	red		orange		yellow		green			blue			purple	

11 Aqueous ammonia is MOST likely to turn universal indicator

  (A) red   Ⓐ

  (B) yellow   Ⓑ

  (C) green   Ⓒ

  (D) blue   Ⓓ

12 Which of the following MOST accurately represents the reaction occurring when calcium hydroxide is heated in a test tube with ammonium sulfate?

  (A) $Ca(OH)_2(aq) + (NH_4)_2SO_4(aq) \longrightarrow CaSO_4(aq) + 2NH_4OH(aq)$ Ⓐ

  (B) $Ca(OH)_2(s) + (NH_4)_2SO_4(s) \longrightarrow CaSO_4(s) + 2NH_4OH(aq)$ Ⓑ

  (C) $Ca(OH)_2(aq) + (NH_4)_2SO_4(aq) \longrightarrow CaSO_4(aq) + 2NH_3(g) + H_2O(l)$ Ⓒ

  (D) $Ca(OH)_2(s) + (NH_4)_2SO_4(s) \longrightarrow CaSO_4(s) + 2NH_3(g) + 2H_2O(l)$ Ⓓ

13 Compound X is insoluble in water, but dissolves in both hydrochloric acid and aqueous sodium hydroxide solution to form colourless solutions. Compound X is possibly

(A) aluminium oxide   Ⓐ

(B) calcium oxide   Ⓑ

(C) magnesium hydroxide   Ⓒ

(D) copper(II) hydroxide   Ⓓ

14 Which of the following correctly classifies the oxides listed?

	Acidic oxide	Basic oxide	Neutral oxide	
(A)	Sulfur trioxide	Calcium oxide	Aluminium oxide	Ⓐ
(B)	Sulfur dioxide	Calcium oxide	Carbon dioxide	Ⓑ
(C)	Sulfur dioxide	Magnesium oxide	Carbon monoxide	Ⓒ
(D)	Nitrogen dioxide	Zinc oxide	Carbon monoxide	Ⓓ

A9 Acids, Bases and Salts (2)

Items **1–2** refer to the following salts.

(A) $NaHSO_4$

(B) $AgCl$

(C) $CaCl_2$

(D) $MgSO_4.7H_2O$

Match EACH item below with one of the options above. Each option may be used once, more than once or not at all.

1 Is an acid salt?

(A)   Ⓐ

(B)   Ⓑ

(C)   Ⓒ

(D)   Ⓓ

2 Is a hydrated salt?

(A)   Ⓐ

(B)   Ⓑ

(C)   Ⓒ

(D)   Ⓓ

3 The following combinations are correct EXCEPT

	Soluble in water	Insoluble in water	
(A)	Lead(II) nitrate	Magnesium carbonate	Ⓐ
(B)	Calcium chloride	Barium sulfate	Ⓑ
(C)	Sodium phosphate	Lead(II) chloride	Ⓒ
(D)	Silver chloride	Lead(II) sulfate	Ⓓ

4 Which of the following salts could NOT be formed from phosphoric acid?

(A) Na_2HPO_4 Ⓐ

(B) NaH_2PO_4 Ⓑ

(C) $NaHPO_4$ Ⓒ

(D) Na_3PO_4 Ⓓ

Item 5 refers to the diagram below, which shows the steps in the preparation of a salt.

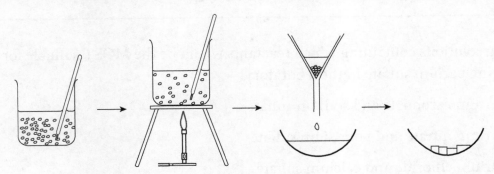

5. For making which salt would the method shown be MOST suitable?

(A) Calcium carbonate   Ⓐ

(B) Potassium nitrate   Ⓑ

(C) Magnesium sulfate   Ⓒ

(D) Anhydrous aluminium chloride   Ⓓ

6. Which salt could NOT be made using a titration?

(A) Calcium nitrate   Ⓐ

(B) Sodium sulfate   Ⓑ

(C) Potassium hydrogensulfate   Ⓒ

(D) Ammonium chloride   Ⓓ

7. Which of the following would be suitable to use to make copper(II) chloride in the laboratory?

    I Copper and hydrochloric acid

    II Copper(II) oxide and hydrochloric acid

    III Copper(II) carbonate and hydrochloric acid

    IV Copper(II) nitrate and hydrochloric acid

(A) I and IV only   Ⓐ

(B) II and III only   Ⓑ

(C) I, II and III only   Ⓒ

(D) II, III and IV only   Ⓓ

8 Mixing solutions containing which reactants would be the MOST suitable for preparing barium sulfate in the laboratory?

(A) Barium carbonate and sodium sulfate Ⓐ

(B) Barium nitrate and potassium sulfate Ⓑ

(C) Barium chloride and calcium sulfate Ⓒ

(D) Barium phosphate and ammonium sulfate Ⓓ

9 During a titration, 20 cm^3 of sulfuric acid neutralised 25 cm^3 of sodium hydroxide solution to make sodium sulfate. What volume of acid would be needed to make sodium hydrogensulfate using 25 cm^3 of sodium hydroxide solution?

(A) 10 cm^3 Ⓐ

(B) 20 cm^3 Ⓑ

(C) 40 cm^3 Ⓒ

(D) 80 cm^3 Ⓓ

10 Which of the following is/are correct?

    I Calcium carbonate is used to make plaster of Paris for orthopaedic casts.

    II Sodium nitrate is used to preserve meat.

    III Magnesium sulfate is used to reduce inflammation.

(A) II only Ⓐ

(B) I and III only Ⓑ

(C) II and III only Ⓒ

(D) I, II and III Ⓓ

11 Consumption of too much of the following salts has been implicated in causing a risk to human health, EXCEPT

(A) sodium chloride Ⓐ

(B) sodium hydrogencarbonate Ⓑ

(C) sodium nitrate Ⓒ

(D) sodium benzoate Ⓓ

Item **12** refers to the graph below, which shows the results of a thermometric titration carried out by adding hydrochloric acid to 25 cm^3 of sodium hydroxide solution.

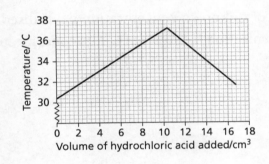

12 The volume of hydrochloric acid needed to neutralise 25 cm^3 of sodium hydroxide solution is

(A) 10.2 cm^3 Ⓐ

(B) 10.4 cm^3 Ⓑ

(C) 16.8 cm^3 Ⓒ

(D) 37.2 cm^3 Ⓓ

13 Which of the following statements is correct?

(A) Farmers and gardeners sometimes add lime to the soil to neutralise any alkalis present. Ⓐ

(B) Toothpaste often contains sodium monofluorophosphate to neutralise any acid in the mouth. Ⓑ

(C) Adding an ammonium fertiliser to the soil at the same time as lime improves the effectiveness of the lime. Ⓒ

(D) Some antacids contain sodium hydrogencarbonate to neutralise stomach acid. Ⓓ

14 30 cm^3 of alkali X of concentration 1.5 mol dm^{-3} requires 15 cm^3 of acid Y of concentration 1.0 mol dm^{-3} for neutralisation. The mole ratio in which the reactants combine is

(A) 3 mol X : 1 mol Y   Ⓐ

(B) 2 mol X : 1 mol Y   Ⓑ

(C) 1 mol X : 2 mol Y   Ⓒ

(D) 1 mol X : 3 mol Y   Ⓓ

15 20 cm^3 of sulfuric acid of unknown concentration neutralised 25 cm^3 sodium hydroxide solution of molar concentration 0.4 mol dm^{-3}. The concentration of the acid was

(A) 0.15 mol dm^{-3} Ⓐ

(B) 0.25 mol dm^{-3} Ⓑ

(C) 0.35 mol dm^{-3} Ⓒ

(D) 0.45 mol dm^{-3} Ⓓ

A10 Oxidation-reduction Reactions

1 Which of the following is NOT an example of oxidation?

(A) The cut surface of an apple turning brown   Ⓐ

(B) A piece of iron rusting   Ⓑ

(C) Respiration in the human body   Ⓒ

(D) Photosynthesis in green plants   Ⓓ

2 During reduction, an element

(A) loses electrons   Ⓐ

(B) gains electrons   Ⓑ

(C) loses protons   Ⓒ

(D) gains protons   Ⓓ

3 Which of the following represent(s) oxidation?

    I $2I^-(aq) \longrightarrow I_2(aq) + 2e^-$

    II $Cu^{2+}(aq) + 2e^- \longrightarrow Cu(s)$

    III $Cl_2(g) + 2e^- \longrightarrow 2Cl^-(s)$

(A) I only   Ⓐ

(B) I and II only   Ⓑ

(C) II and III only   Ⓒ

(D) I, II and III   Ⓓ

4 Which of the following is an example of reduction?

(A) The conversion of calcium atoms to calcium ions   Ⓐ

(B) The conversion of bromide ions to bromine   Ⓑ

(C) The conversion of iron(II) ions to iron(III) ions   Ⓒ

(D) The conversion of sulfur atoms to sulfide ions   Ⓓ

5 Which of the following is/are true?

    I The oxidation number of the aluminium ion is always +3.

    II The oxidation number of oxygen in covalent compounds is always –2.

    III The oxidation number of uncombined magnesium is always +2.

(A) I only   Ⓐ

(B) I and III only   Ⓑ

(C) II and III only   Ⓒ

(D) I, II and III   Ⓓ

6 The oxidation number of chlorine in the ClO_3^- ion is

(A) +3   Ⓐ

(B) +4   Ⓑ

(C) +5   Ⓒ

(D) +6   Ⓓ

7 The (VI) after dichromate in the dichromate(VI) ion refers to

(A) the charge on the ion $\quad$ Ⓐ

(B) the oxidation number of the ion $\quad$ Ⓑ

(C) the oxidation number of chromium in the ion $\quad$ Ⓒ

(D) the oxidation number of oxygen in the ion $\quad$ Ⓓ

8 In which reaction does sulfur show the GREATEST increase in oxidation number?

(A) $S(g) + O_2(g) \longrightarrow SO_2(g)$ $\quad$ Ⓐ

(B) $2SO_2(g) + O_2(g) \longrightarrow 2SO_3(g)$ $\quad$ Ⓑ

(C) $H_2S(g) + O_2(g) \longrightarrow 3H_2O(l) + 2S(s)$ $\quad$ Ⓒ

(D) $FeS(s) + 2HCl(aq) \longrightarrow FeCl_2(s) + H_2S(g)$ $\quad$ Ⓓ

9 In a redox reaction, the oxidation number of the element that is oxidised always

(A) increases by 1 $\quad$ Ⓐ

(B) increases $\quad$ Ⓑ

(C) decreases $\quad$ Ⓒ

(D) remains unchanged $\quad$ Ⓓ

10 Which of the following is NOT a redox reaction?

(A) $KOH(aq) + HCl(aq) \longrightarrow KCl(aq) + H_2O(l)$ $\quad$ Ⓐ

(B) $Zn(s) + CuSO_4(aq) \longrightarrow ZnSO_4(aq) + Cu(s)$ $\quad$ Ⓑ

(C) $2H_2(g) + O_2(g) \longrightarrow 2H_2O(g)$ $\quad$ Ⓒ

(D) $2FeCl_2(s) + Cl_2(g) \longrightarrow 2FeCl_3(s)$ $\quad$ Ⓓ

11 Which substance has been oxidised in the following reaction?

$$Cl_2(g) + 2KBr(aq) \longrightarrow 2KCl(aq) + Br_2(aq)$$

(A) Chlorine (A)

(B) Potassium bromide (B)

(C) Potassium chloride (C)

(D) Bromine (D)

12 A reducing agent always

(A) causes a loss of electrons (A)

(B) causes a colour change during a reaction (B)

(C) gains electrons (C)

(D) causes a decrease in oxidation number (D)

13 Which of the following could be used to confirm that a colourless solution, X, is a reducing agent?

    I Acidified hydrogen peroxide solution

    II Acidified potassium dichromate(VI) solution

    III Acidified potassium manganate(VII) solution

(A) I only (A)

(B) I and III only (B)

(C) II and III only (C)

(D) I, II and III (D)

14 In two separate experiments, sulfur dioxide was bubbled through acidified potassium manganate(VII) solution and acidified potassium dichromate(VI) solution. Which colour changes were observed in the solutions?

	Acidified potassium manganate(VII) solution	Acidified potassium dichromate(VI) solution	
(A)	Orange to green	Purple to colourless	(A)
(B)	Purple to colourless	Green to orange	(B)
(C)	Purple to colourless	Orange to green	(C)
(D)	Colourless to purple	Green to orange	(D)

15 Acidified hydrogen peroxide can

    I oxidise potassium iodide solution

    II reduce acidified potassium manganate(VII) solution

    III turn green iron(II) sulfate solution yellow

(A) I only   Ⓐ

(B) I and III only   Ⓑ

(C) II and III only   Ⓒ

(D) I, II and III   Ⓓ

16 Which statement is true about the following reaction?

$$Mg(s) + H_2SO_4(aq) \longrightarrow MgSO_4(aq) + H_2(g)$$

(A) Magnesium has been reduced.   Ⓐ

(B) The H^+ ions in the sulfuric acid lost electrons.   Ⓑ

(C) Sulfuric acid is the oxidising agent.   Ⓒ

(D) The oxidation number of magnesium changed from +2 to 0.   Ⓓ

A11 Electrochemistry

1 Metal Y reacts with hydrochloric acid but remains unchanged when placed in a solution containing the nitrate of metal X. From this it can be deduced that

(A) Y is higher in the electrochemical series than X   Ⓐ

(B) Y is higher in the electrochemical series than hydrogen   Ⓑ

(C) Y is a stronger reducing agent than X   Ⓒ

(D) Y is a weaker reducing agent than hydrogen.   Ⓓ

2 Which of the following reactions is likely to take place LEAST easily?

(A) $Mg(s) + Cu(NO_3)_2(aq) \longrightarrow Mg(NO_3)_2(aq) + Cu(s)$ Ⓐ

(B) $Mg(s) + 2AgNO_3(aq) \longrightarrow Mg(NO_3)_2(aq) + 2Ag(s)$ Ⓑ

(C) $Mg(s) + Zn(NO_3)_2(aq) \longrightarrow Mg(NO_3)_2(aq) + Zn(s)$ Ⓒ

(D) $Mg(s) + Fe(NO_3)_2(aq) \longrightarrow Mg(NO_3)_2(aq) + Fe(s)$ Ⓓ

3 All of the following are electrolytes EXCEPT

(A) molten sodium chloride Ⓐ

(B) dilute hydrochloric acid Ⓑ

(C) ethanol Ⓒ

(D) tap water Ⓓ

Item 4 refers to the following apparatus, which was set up to investigate the conductivity of four solutions.

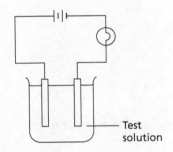

Test solution

4 Which solution would cause the light bulb to glow the brightest?

(A) Aqueous hydrochloric acid Ⓐ

(B) Aqueous ethanoic acid Ⓑ

(C) Aqueous ammonia Ⓒ

(D) Glucose solution Ⓓ

5 Which of the following correctly summarises metallic and electrolytic conduction?

	Metallic conduction	**Electrolytic conduction**	
(A)	Mobile ions carry the electric current	The electrolyte decomposes	Ⓐ
(B)	Mobile ions carry the electric current	The electrolyte remains chemically unchanged	Ⓑ
(C)	Mobile electrons carry the electric current	The electrolyte remains chemically unchanged	Ⓒ
(D)	Mobile electrons carry the electric current	The electrolyte decomposes	Ⓓ

6 The reaction occurring at the cathode during electrolysis is

(A) oxidation   Ⓐ

(B) reduction   Ⓑ

(C) displacement   Ⓒ

(D) ionisation   Ⓓ

7 If molten lead(II) bromide is electrolysed using graphite electrodes

(A) red-brown fumes of bromine are seen at the cathode   Ⓐ

(B) solid lead forms around the anode   Ⓑ

(C) molten lead drips off the cathode   Ⓒ

(D) the anode decreases in size   Ⓓ

8 Which factor does NOT influence the preferential discharge of an ion at the anode during electrolysis of an aqueous electrolyte?

(A) The position of the ion in the electrochemical series   Ⓐ

(B) The strength of the electrolyte   Ⓑ

(C) The type of anode   Ⓒ

(D) The concentration of the electrolyte   Ⓓ

9 Which ions move towards the anode when copper(II) sulfate solution is being electrolysed?

(A) Cu^{2+} ions only

(B) Cu^{2+} and H^+ ions

(C) OH^- ions only

(D) OH^- and SO_4^{2-} ions

Item 10 refers to the electrolytic cell shown below.

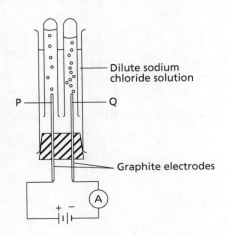

10 Which of the following correctly identifies the gases evolved at P and Q?

	P	Q	
(A)	Oxygen	Hydrogen	Ⓐ
(B)	Chlorine	Hydrogen	Ⓑ
(C)	Hydrogen	Chlorine	Ⓒ
(D)	Hydrogen	Oxygen	Ⓓ

11 Which of the following observation(s) would a student expect to make during the electrolysis of copper(II) sulfate solution using copper electrodes?

    I The electrolyte becomes paler blue.

    II The anode decreases in size.

    III Pink copper is deposited around the cathode.

(A) I only   Ⓐ

(B) I and III only   Ⓑ

(C) II and III only   Ⓒ

(D) I, II and III   Ⓓ

12 During the electrolysis of concentrated hydrochloric acid using graphite electrodes:

(A) oxygen is evolved.   Ⓐ

(B) chlorine is evolved.   Ⓑ

(C) hydrogen chloride is evolved.   Ⓒ

(D) the electrolyte becomes more acidic.   Ⓓ

<u>Items **13–14**</u> refer to the following electrolytic cell.

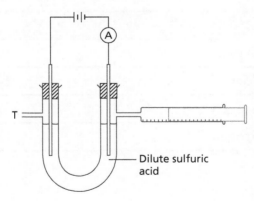

T

Dilute sulfuric acid

13 Which equation accurately summarises the reaction occurring at the anode?

(A) $2H^+(aq) + 2e^- \longrightarrow H_2(g)$ Ⓐ

(B) $SO_4^{2-}(aq) \longrightarrow S(s) + 2O_2(g) + 2e^-$ Ⓑ

(C) $2O^{2-}(aq) \longrightarrow O_2(g) + 4e^-$ Ⓒ

(D) $4OH^-(aq) \longrightarrow 2H_2O(l) + O_2(g) + 4e^-$ Ⓓ

14 After 15 minutes, the volume of gas collected in the gas syringe was 50.0 cm^3. If a gas syringe had also been placed at T, what volume of gas would have been collected in this syringe?'

(A) 12.5 cm^3 Ⓐ

(B) 25.0 cm^3 Ⓑ

(C) 50.0 cm^3 Ⓒ

(D) 100.0 cm^3 Ⓓ

15 What mass of copper would be deposited at the cathode if a current of 2.5 A flows through copper(II) sulfate solution for 51 minutes and 28 seconds?

(A) 1.28 g   Ⓐ

(B) 2.56 g   Ⓑ

(C) 5.12 g   Ⓒ

(D) 10.24 g   Ⓓ

16 What quantity of electricity would be required to deposit 0.1 mol of chromium during the process of chrome plating using chromium(III) sulfate solution?

(A) 9650 C   Ⓐ

(B) 19 300 C   Ⓑ

(C) 28 950 C   Ⓒ

(D) 96 500 C   Ⓓ

17 During electrolysis, 96 500 C of electricity produced 0.5 mol of element X at the cathode of one electrolytic cell and 1.0 mol of element Y at the cathode of another electrolytic cell. The ions of X and Y can be written as follows.

(A) X^{2+}, Y^+ Ⓐ

(B) X^+, Y^{2+} Ⓑ

(C) X^{2-}, Y^- Ⓒ

(D) X^-, Y^{2-} Ⓓ

18 Which metal could NOT be purified by electrolysis?

(A) Copper   Ⓐ

(B) Silver   Ⓑ

(C) Gold   Ⓒ

(D) Iron   Ⓓ

19 Which of the following is/are uses of electrolysis?

    I To protect an aluminium saucepan against corrosion

    II To extract aluminium from its ore

    III To coat a steel spoon with a thin layer of aluminium

(A) II only   Ⓐ

(B) I and II only   Ⓑ

(C) I and III only   Ⓒ

(D) I, II and III   Ⓓ

20 During the electroplating of a trophy with silver, the reaction occurring at the cathode is

(A) $Ag^+(aq) + e^- \longrightarrow Ag(s)$ Ⓐ

(B) $Ag^{2+}(aq) + 2e^- \longrightarrow Ag(s)$ Ⓑ

(C) $Ag(s) \longrightarrow Ag^+(aq) + e^-$ Ⓒ

(D) $Ag(s) \longrightarrow Ag^{2+}(aq) + 2e^-$ Ⓓ

1 Which of the following can be used to accurately measure the rate of reaction between calcium carbonate chips and hydrochloric acid?

    I The decrease in mass of the reaction over time

    II The decrease in volume of the reactants over time

    III The increase in volume of gas produced over time

(A) II only   Ⓐ

(B) I and III only   Ⓑ

(C) II and III only   Ⓒ

(D) I, II and III   Ⓓ

2 Which of the following is NOT necessary for a chemical reaction to occur?

(A) The particles of the reactants must collide   Ⓐ

(B) Bonds must break in the reactants   Ⓑ

(C) The particles of the reactants must collide with a certain minimum energy   Ⓒ

(D) The particles of the products must collide with the correct orientation   Ⓓ

<u>Item 3</u> refers to the following apparatus, which can be used to study the rate of reaction between magnesium carbonate and nitric acid.

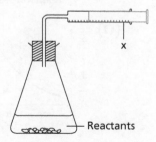

3 X is MOST correctly called

(A) a glass syringe   Ⓐ

(B) a gas measuring device   Ⓑ

(C) a gas syringe   Ⓒ

(D) a syringe   Ⓓ

4 The following factors affect the rate of reaction between zinc and hydrochloric acid EXCEPT

(A) the concentration of the acid (A)

(B) the volume of the acid (B)

(C) the temperature of the acid (C)

(D) the particle size of the zinc (D)

5 During a chemical reaction in which a catalyst is used

(A) the mass of the catalyst remains unchanged (A)

(B) the chemical composition of the catalyst changes (B)

(C) the mass of the catalyst decreases (C)

(D) the appearance of the catalyst changes (D)

6 Which graph below BEST shows how the rate of a reaction varies with temperature?

(A)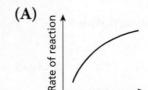

(B)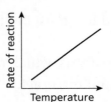

(A)
(B)
(C)
(D)

(C)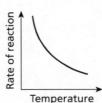

(D)

7 Activation energy is the minimum amount of energy that

(A) products must possess at the end of the reaction (A)

(B) must be supplied to reactant particles (B)

(C) particles must collide with in order to react (C)

(D) reactant particles must produce as they move around (D)

8 Which of the following BEST explains why flour mills need to be kept cool and well ventilated?

(A) Flour is flammable. Ⓐ

(B) Flour stays fresher if it is stored in cool conditions. Ⓑ

(C) Finely divided flour particles can ignite spontaneously if temperatures are too high. Ⓒ

(D) Finely divided flour particles clump together if temperatures are too high. Ⓓ

9 During a chemical reaction, an increase in temperature

I increases the kinetic energy of particles

II causes particles to collide less frequently

III increases the speed of movement of particles

IV causes particles to collide with less energy

(A) I and III only Ⓐ

(B) II and III only Ⓑ

(C) II and IV only Ⓒ

(D) I, II and III only Ⓓ

10 In experiment (i), 10.0 g of magnesium ribbon reacts with excess sulfuric acid at room temperature, and the reaction flask is weighed at regular intervals. The method is then repeated in experiment (ii) using 10.0 g of magnesium powder in place of the ribbon. Which graph BEST illustrates the results of the two experiments?

(A)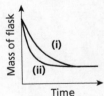

(B)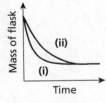

Ⓐ
Ⓑ
Ⓒ
Ⓓ

(C)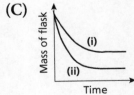

(D)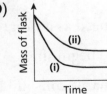

11 A catalyst speeds up a chemical reaction by

(A) taking part in the reaction Ⓐ

(B) lowering the activation energy of the reaction Ⓑ

(C) supplying heat energy to the reaction Ⓒ

(D) providing an alternative pathway for the reaction, which requires Ⓓ
a lower activation energy.

12 When excess hydrochloric acid is added to a solution of sodium thiosulfate, a pale yellow precipitate of sulfur forms. If the experiment is repeated, increasing the volume of acid added but not changing its concentration

(A) the rate at which the sulfur forms decreases Ⓐ

(B) the rate at which the sulfur forms increases Ⓑ

(C) sulfur forms at the same rate Ⓒ

(D) no precipitate of sulfur forms Ⓓ

Items **13–15** refer to the graph below, which shows the results of an experiment carried out to measure how the rate of reaction between calcium carbonate and excess hydrochloric acid varies with time. The reaction was carried out at room temperature and pressure.

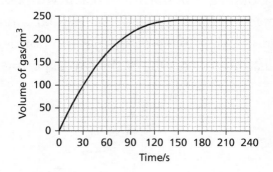

13 The graph shows that

(A) the reaction increases in speed as it progresses Ⓐ

(B) the reaction is fastest at the beginning Ⓑ

(C) the rate of the reaction remains constant throughout Ⓒ

(D) the reaction reaches completion after 240 s Ⓓ

14 The average rate of reaction in the first minute was

(A) $2.57 \text{ cm}^3 \text{ s}^{-1}$ (A)

(B) $2.83 \text{ cm}^3 \text{ s}^{-1}$ (B)

(C) $5.67 \text{ cm}^3 \text{ s}^{-1}$ (C)

(D) $170.0 \text{ cm}^3 \text{ s}^{-1}$ (D)

15 How many moles of hydrochloric acid were used in the reaction?

(A) 0.005 mol (A)

(B) 0.01 mol (B)

(C) 0.02 mol (C)

(D) 0.04 mol (D)

A13 Energetics

1 Which of the following statements about a chemical reaction is/are correct?

   I Energy is absorbed from the surroundings to break bonds.

   II Forming bonds is an endothermic process.

   III More energy is involved in breaking bonds than in forming bonds.

(A) I only (A)

(B) I and II only (B)

(C) II and III only (C)

(D) I, II and III (D)

2 Which of the following combinations is correct?

	Exothermic reaction	Endothermic reaction	
(A)	Absorbs energy from the surroundings	The temperature of the reaction mixture decreases	Ⓐ
(B)	Releases energy to the surroundings	The temperature of the reaction mixture increases	Ⓑ
(C)	The temperature of the reaction mixture decreases	Releases energy to the surroundings	Ⓒ
(D)	The temperature of the reaction mixture increases	Absorbs energy from the surroundings	Ⓓ

3 Which of the following is an endothermic reaction?

(A) Combustion   Ⓐ

(B) Photosynthesis   Ⓑ

(C) Neutralisation   Ⓒ

(D) Respiration   Ⓓ

4 A student was asked to write down FOUR pieces of information that could be obtained from the following equation.

$$Mg(s) + CuSO_4(aq) \longrightarrow MgSO_4(aq) + Cu(s) \qquad \Delta H \text{ } -ve$$

Which of the following pieces of information is NOT correct?

(A) Copper(II) sulfate and magnesium sulfate are both soluble in water.   Ⓐ

(B) The reaction is exothermic.   Ⓑ

(C) The total energy content of the products is less than the total energy content of the reactants.   Ⓒ

(D) The temperature of the reaction decreases.   Ⓓ

Items <u>5–7</u> refer to the following energy profile diagram.

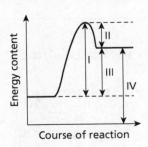

5 Which statement about the reaction is correct?

(A) ΔH is positive.

(B) The reactants contain more energy than the products.

(C) The reaction is exothermic.

(D) Less energy is absorbed to break bonds in the reactants than is released when new bonds are formed in the products.

Ⓐ

Ⓑ

Ⓒ

Ⓓ

6 Which arrow represents the change in enthalpy of the reaction?

(A) I

(B) II

(C) III

(D) IV

Ⓐ

Ⓑ

Ⓒ

Ⓓ

7 Which arrow represents the energy that the reactants must be given to begin forming products?

(A) I

(B) II

(C) III

(D) IV

Ⓐ

Ⓑ

Ⓒ

Ⓓ

8 Which diagram below correctly shows the effect of a catalyst on a chemical reaction?

(A)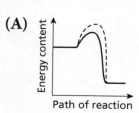

(B)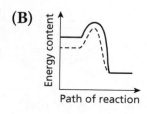

(C)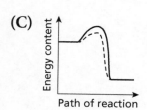

(D)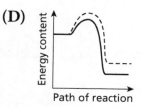

— Uncatalysed reaction

---- Catalysed reaction

9 When measuring the enthalpy change during an endothermic reaction, a calorimeter is used to

    I prevent heat being absorbed from the environment

    II act as a container for the reactants

    III prevent heat being lost to the environment

(A) I only

(B) I and II only

(C) II and III only

(D) I, II and III

Ⓐ

Ⓑ

Ⓒ

Ⓓ

10 When sodium hydroxide dissolves in water, which of the following energy changes occur?

    I Absorption of energy to break intermolecular forces between water molecules

    II Absorption of energy to break intermolecular forces between ions

    III Release of energy as ions are attracted to water molecules

(A) II only

(B) I and II only

(C) I and III only

(D) I, II and III

11 The heats of solution of three compounds are given in the table below.

Compound	Heat of solution/ kJ mol^{-1}
Potassium chloride	+17.25
Ammonium nitrate	+25.69
Ethanol	−5.27

Which of the following CANNOT be deduced from the information in the table?

(A) Dissolving potassium chloride and ammonium nitrate are both endothermic processes.

(B) Less energy is absorbed to break the intermolecular forces between ethanol molecules and the water molecules than is released during solvation.

(C) As ethanol dissolves the temperature of the solution would increase.

(D) It takes more energy to break ionic bonds than intermolecular forces.

12 25 cm^3 of 1.0 mol dm^{-3} hydrochloric acid is added to 25 cm^3 of 1.0 mol dm^{-3} aqueous potassium hydroxide and a temperature increase of 6.5 °C is recorded. Assuming that the specific heat capacity of the solution is 4.2 J g^{-1} °C^{-1}, the heat change for the reaction is:

(A) $\dfrac{25 \times 25 \times 4.2 \times 6.5}{1000}$ kJ

(B) $25 \times 25 \times 4.2 \times 6.5$ kJ

(C) $50 \times 4.2 \times 6.5$ kJ

(D) $\dfrac{50 \times 4.2 \times 6.5}{1000}$ kJ

13 Aqueous sodium hydroxide reacts with nitric acid according to the following equation.

$$NaOH(aq) + HNO_3(aq) \longrightarrow NaNO_3(aq) + H_2O(l) \qquad \Delta H = -57 \text{ kJ mol}^{-1}$$

From this it can be deduced that 114 kJ of energy would be released when

(A) 1 mol sodium hydroxide reacts with 2 mol nitric acid   Ⓐ

(B) 2 mol sodium hydroxide react with 1 mol nitric acid   Ⓑ

(C) 2 mol sodium hydroxide react with 2 mol nitric acid   Ⓒ

(D) 3 mol sodium hydroxide react with 2 mol nitric acid   Ⓓ

14 When 500 cm^3 of 1.0 mol dm^{-3} of sodium hydroxide solution was neutralised by 500 cm^3 of 1.0 mol dm^{-3} hydrochloric acid, 28.4 kJ of energy was evolved. The same amount of energy would be evolved by mixing

	Alkali	Acid
I	500 cm^3 of 1.0 mol dm^{-3} sodium hydroxide solution	500 cm^3 of 1.0 mol dm^{-3} ethanoic acid
II	500 cm^3 of 1.0 mol dm^{-3} potassium hydroxide solution	500 cm^3 of 1.0 mol dm^{-3} hydrochloric acid
III	500 cm^3 of 1.0 mol dm^{-3} potassium hydroxide solution	500 cm^3 of 1.0 mol dm^{-3} nitric acid
IV	500 cm^3 of 1.0 mol dm^{-3} ammonia solution	500 cm^3 of 1.0 mol dm^{-3} hydrochloric acid

(A) I and II only   Ⓐ

(B) II and III only   Ⓑ

(C) III and IV only   Ⓒ

(D) I and IV only   Ⓓ

15 The following equation summarises the combustion of ethane.

$$C_2H_4(g) + 3O_2(g) \longrightarrow 2CO_2(g) + 2H_2O(g) \qquad \Delta H = -1411 \text{ kJ mol}^{-1}$$

Which energy profile diagram MOST accurately represents the reaction?

(A)

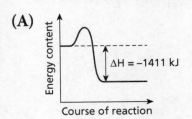

(B)

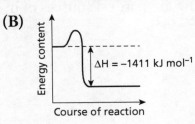

(C)

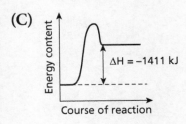

(D)

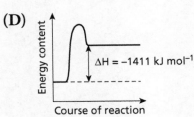

Section B: Organic Chemistry
B1 Sources of Hydrocarbon Compounds

1 Which of the following are natural sources of hydrocarbons?

    I Petroleum

    II Coal

    III Natural gas

    IV Charcoal

(A) I and III only   Ⓐ

(B) II and IV only   Ⓑ

(C) I, II and III only   Ⓒ

(D) II, III and IV only   Ⓓ

2 The different components of crude oil are separated due to their different

(A) melting points   Ⓐ

(B) densities   Ⓑ

(C) solubilities   Ⓒ

(D) boiling points   Ⓓ

3 The hydrocarbons present in natural gas include

(A) methane, propane and butane   Ⓐ

(B) ethane, butane and pentane   Ⓑ

(C) methane, ethane and pentane   Ⓒ

(D) methane, propane and hexane   Ⓓ

Items **4–5** refer to the following fractionating tower. In answering the items, each option may be used once, more than once or not at all.

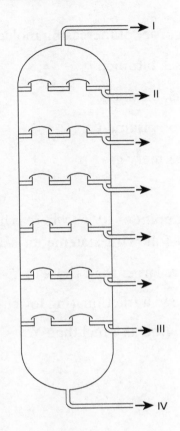

4 Which fraction is MOST likely to be petrol?

(A) I

(B) II

(C) III

(D) IV

Ⓐ

Ⓑ

Ⓒ

Ⓓ

5 Which fraction is MOST likely to be used as lubricants?

(A) I

(B) II

(C) III

(D) IV

Ⓐ

Ⓑ

Ⓒ

Ⓓ

6 Which list shows the correct order of increasing molecular size?

(A) Refinery gas, petrol, diesel, bitumen

(B) Petrol, refinery gas, diesel, bitumen

(C) Refinery gas, diesel, petrol, bitumen

(D) Bitumen, diesel, petrol, refinery gas

Ⓐ
Ⓑ
Ⓒ
Ⓓ

7 Hydrocarbon X has a boiling point of 10 °C, whereas hydrocarbon Y has a boiling point of 420 °C. Which of the following statements is/are true?

    I The molecules of X are larger than those of Y.

    II X will remain as a gas in a fractionating tower.

    III X is more likely to be used as a fuel than Y.

(A) II only

(B) I and III only

(C) II and III only

(D) I, II and III

Ⓐ
Ⓑ
Ⓒ
Ⓓ

8 Which of the following INCORRECTLY matches the fraction obtained from crude oil with its use?

	Fraction	Use	
(A)	Naphtha	Manufacture petrochemicals	Ⓐ
(B)	Bitumen	Surfacing roads	Ⓑ
(C)	Refinery gas	Fuel for power stations	Ⓒ
(D)	Kerosene	Fuel for jet engines	Ⓓ

The following statements are correct EXCEPT

(A) Hydrocarbons can be cracked by applying heat, or heat and a catalyst. Ⓐ

(B) During cracking, carbon-carbon double bonds are broken. Ⓑ

(C) Cracking hydrocarbons increases the availability of useful molecules. Ⓒ

(D) Cracking hydrocarbons always produces at least one alkene. Ⓓ

Item 10 refers to the following hydrocarbon.

$$H-CH_2-CH_2-CH_2-CH_2-CH_2-CH_2-CH_3$$

(structural formula: a chain of 7 carbons each with H substituents — heptane)

10 Which combination could NOT be obtained from cracking the hydrocarbon illustrated?

(A) $CH_3-CH_2-CH_3$ + $CH_3-CH_2-CH=CH_2$ Ⓐ

(B) CH_3-CH_3 + $CH_3-CH_2-CH_2-CH=CH_2$ Ⓑ

(C) CH_3-CH_3 + $CH_2=CH_2$ + $CH_3-CH=CH_2$ Ⓒ

(D) CH_4 + $CH_3-CH_2-CH_3$ + $CH_3-CH=CH_2$ Ⓓ

1

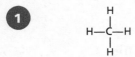

The angle between the covalent bonds in the methane molecule above is

(A) 90.0° (A)

(B) 106.5° (B)

(C) 109.5° (C)

(D) 120.0° (D)

2 The ability of carbon atoms to bond covalently with other carbon atoms to form chains is called

(A) condensation (A)

(B) catenation (B)

(C) addition (C)

(D) polymerisation (D)

3 Which of the following CANNOT be formed when carbon atoms bond with other carbon atoms?

(A) Double bonds between adjacent carbon atoms (A)

(B) Rings of carbon atoms (B)

(C) Branched chains of carbon atoms (C)

(D) Quadruple bonds between adjacent carbon atoms (D)

4 Which of the following is/are characteristics of a homologous series?

     I Members have the same molecular formula

     II Members have the same physical properties

     III Members have the same functional group

(A) III only   Ⓐ

(B) I and II only   Ⓑ

(C) II and III only   Ⓒ

(D) I, II and III   Ⓓ

5 The general formula of an alkene is

(A) C_nH_{2n-1} Ⓐ

(B) C_nH_{2n} Ⓑ

(C) C_nH_{2n+1} Ⓒ

(D) C_nH_{2n+2} Ⓓ

6 The functional group found in members of the alcohol series is the

(A) hydroxyl group   Ⓐ

(B) hydroxide group   Ⓑ

(C) carboxyl group   Ⓒ

(D) amino group   Ⓓ

Items **7–8** refer to the following options. When answering the items, each option may be used once, more than once or not at all.

(A) Alkane series

(B) Alkene series

(C) Alcohol series

(D) Alkanoic acid series

7 To which homologous series does C_4H_{10} belong?

(A)   Ⓐ

(B)   Ⓑ

(C)   Ⓒ

(D)   Ⓓ

8 To which homologous series does a compound composed of 36 g carbon, 8 g hydrogen and 16 g oxygen belong?

(A)   Ⓐ

(B)   Ⓑ

(C)   Ⓒ

(D)   Ⓓ

9 Which could be given as the general formula of the alkanoic acid series?

       I $C_nH_{2n+2}CO_2$

       II $C_nH_{2n+1}COOH$

       III $C_{n+1}H_{2n+2}O_2$

(A) II only   Ⓐ

(B) I and III only   Ⓑ

(C) II and III only   Ⓒ

(D) I, II and III   Ⓓ

10 Which of the following is an alcohol?

(A)

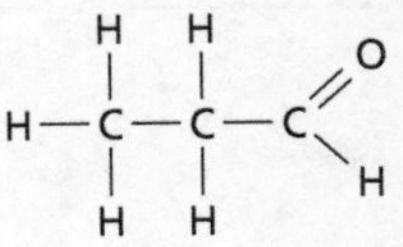

(B)

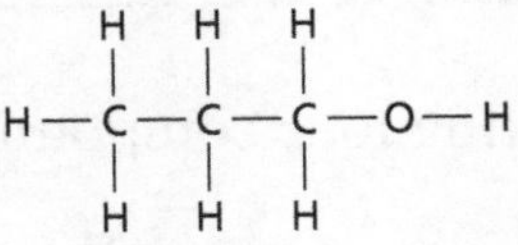

(C)

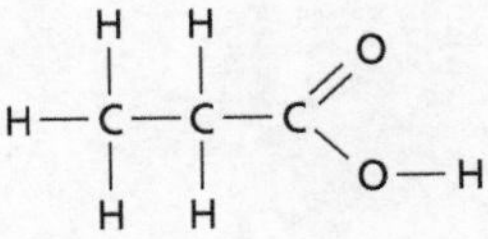

(D)

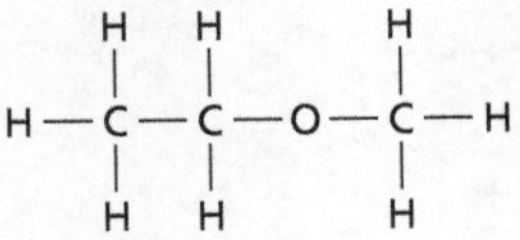

Ⓐ
Ⓑ
Ⓒ
Ⓓ

11 A compound with the molecular formula $C_4H_8O_2$ belongs to the alkanoic acid series. Which is the correct structural formula for the compound?

(A)

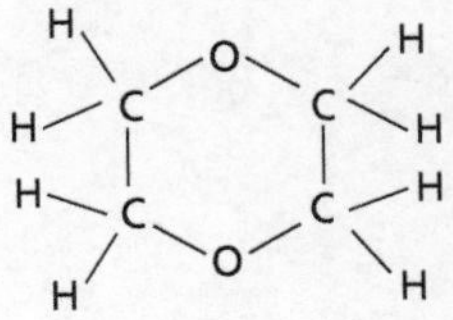

(B)

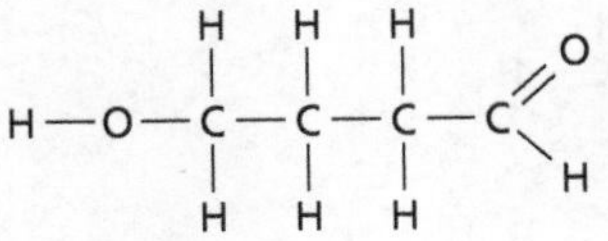

(C)

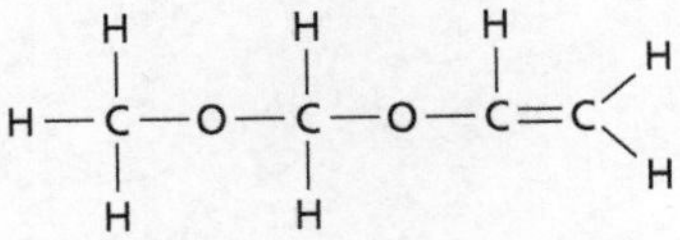

(D)

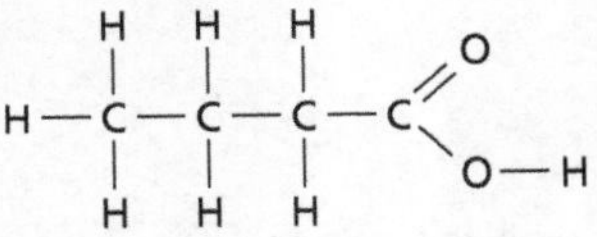

Ⓐ
Ⓑ
Ⓒ
Ⓓ

12 C_2H_5COOH is called

(A) propanoic acid

(B) ethanoic acid

(C) butanoic acid

(D) methanoic acid

Ⓐ
Ⓑ
Ⓒ
Ⓓ

13 Structural isomers of a compound with the molecular formula C_5H_{12} have

(A) the same chemical properties

(B) the same melting point

(C) different structural formulae

(D) different functional groups

Ⓐ
Ⓑ
Ⓒ
Ⓓ

Item **14** refers to the following four compounds.

I

$$H-\overset{\overset{\displaystyle H}{|}}{\underset{\underset{\displaystyle H}{|}}{C}}-\overset{\overset{\displaystyle H}{|}}{\underset{\underset{\displaystyle H}{|}}{C}}-\overset{\overset{\displaystyle H}{|}}{\underset{\underset{\displaystyle H}{|}}{C}}-\overset{\overset{\displaystyle H}{|}}{\underset{\underset{\displaystyle H}{|}}{C}}-H$$

II

III

IV

14 The following pairs are isomers EXCEPT

(A) I and II

(B) I and IV

(C) II and III

(D) III and IV

Ⓐ
Ⓑ
Ⓒ
Ⓓ

15 Which of the following compounds will exhibit structural isomerism?

(A) CH_4

(B) C_2H_6

(C) C_3H_6

(D) C_4H_8

Ⓐ
Ⓑ
Ⓒ
Ⓓ

16 Three isomers have the molecular formula C_4H_8. The structure of one isomer is

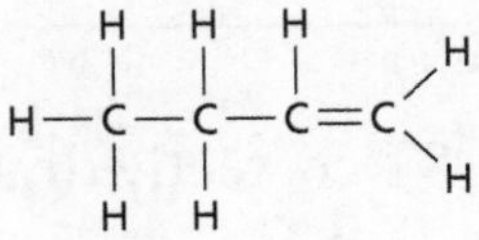

The structure of the other two could be

I

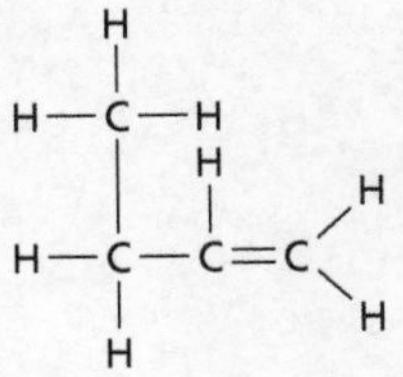

II

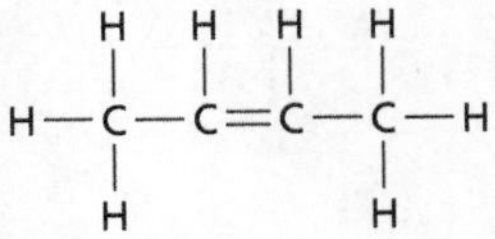

III

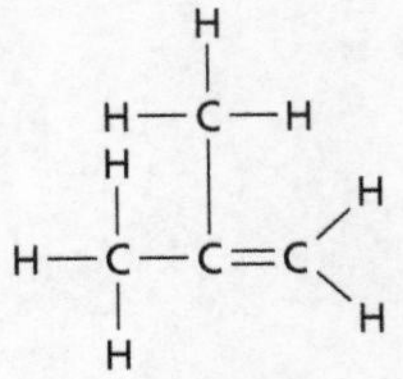

IV

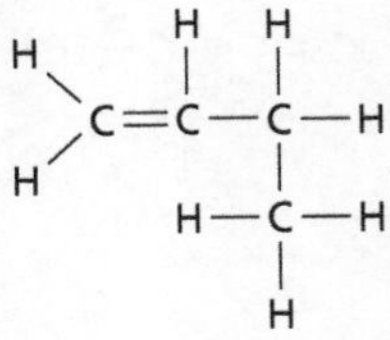

(A) I and II

(B) II and III

(C) III and IV

(D) I and IV

Ⓐ

Ⓑ

Ⓒ

Ⓓ

Item **17** refers to the following compound.

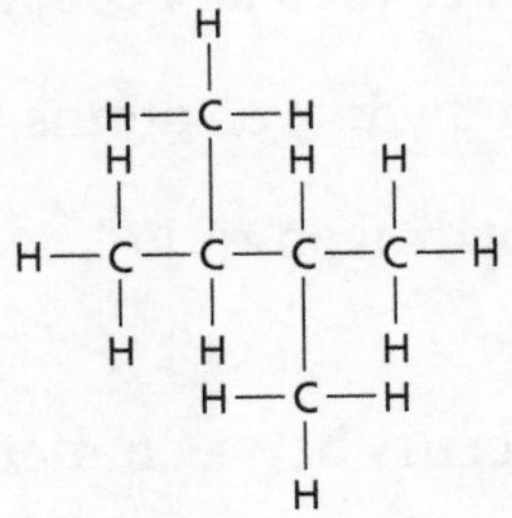

17 The correct name for the compound is

(A) 2,3-dimethylhexane

(B) 3,2-dimethylhexane

(C) 2,3-dimethylbutane

(D) 3,2-dimethylbutane

Ⓐ

Ⓑ

Ⓒ

Ⓓ

B2 Organic Chemistry – An Introduction (cont.)

18 Which of the following is the MOST correctly drawn structural formula of hex-2-ene (2-hexene)?

(A)

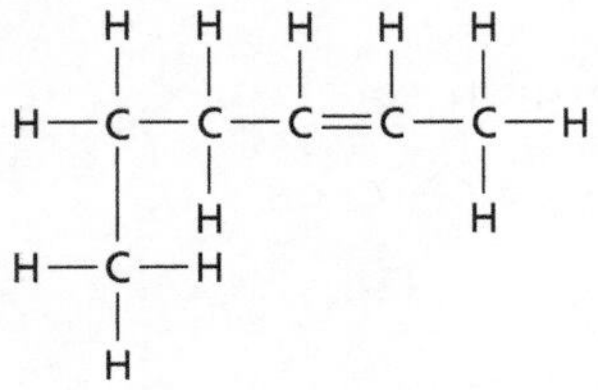

(B)

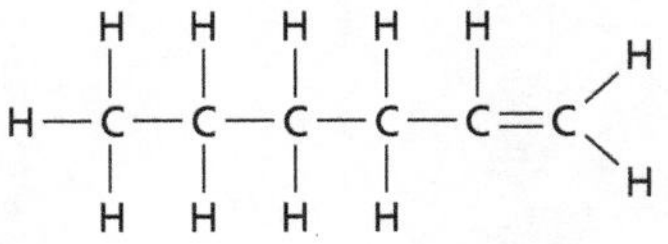

(C)

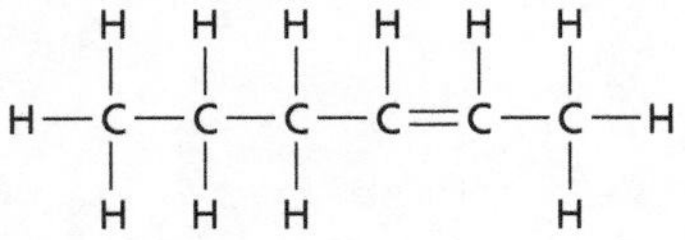

(D)

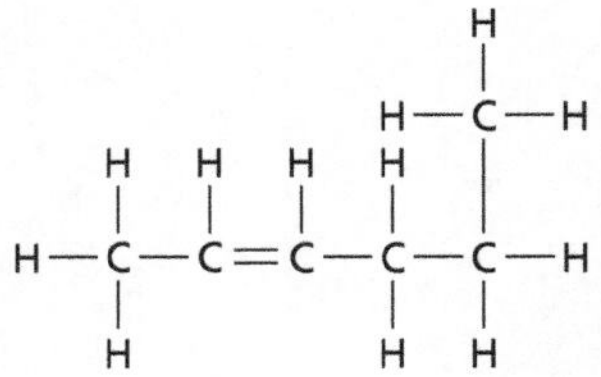

B3 Reactions of Carbon Compounds (1)

1 Alkanes are saturated hydrocarbons because

(A) they contain only carbon and hydrogen atoms

(B) they have only single bonds between adjacent carbon atoms

(C) they can accommodate more hydrogen atoms in their molecules

(D) they have a high carbon to hydrogen ratio

<u>Items 2–3</u> refer to the reaction that occurs between methane and chlorine in dim light.

2 Which of the following would NOT be produced during the reaction?

(A) $CHCl_3$

(B) HCl

(C) H_2

(D) CH_3Cl

3 The reaction is known as

(A) an addition reaction   Ⓐ

(B) a dehydration reaction   Ⓑ

(C) a condensation reaction   Ⓒ

(D) a substitution reaction   Ⓓ

4 When burnt in a plentiful supply of oxygen, which of the following compounds would produce the smokiest flame?

(A) C_2H_5OH Ⓐ

(B) C_2H_6 Ⓑ

(C) C_2H_4 Ⓒ

(D) C_2H_2 Ⓓ

5 Which of the following represents the compound formed when $CH_3CH=CH_2$ reacts with chlorine?

(A)

```
   Cl  H  Cl
   |   |   |
H— C — C — C —H
   |   |   |
   H   H   H
```

(B)

```
   H   H  Cl
   |   |   |
H— C — C — C —Cl
   |   |   |
   H   H   H
```

(C)

```
   H   Cl Cl
   |   |   |
H— C — C — C —H
   |   |   |
   H   H   H
```

(D)

```
   H   Cl  H
   |   |   |
H— C — C — C —H
   |   |   |
   H   Cl  H
```

Ⓐ Ⓑ Ⓒ Ⓓ

6 Which of the following correctly summarises the observations when cyclohexane and cyclohexene are separately added to acidified potassium manganate(VII) solution?

	Cyclohexane	Cyclohexene	
(A)	Remains purple	Colour changes from purple to colourless	Ⓐ
(B)	Colour changes from purple to colourless	Colour changes from purple to colourless	Ⓑ
(C)	Remains purple	Remains purple	Ⓒ
(D)	Colour changes from purple to colourless	Remains purple	Ⓓ

Item <u>7</u> refers to the three compounds below.

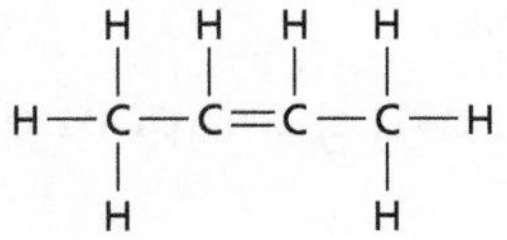

7 Which compound(s) will undergo an addition reaction with hydrogen?

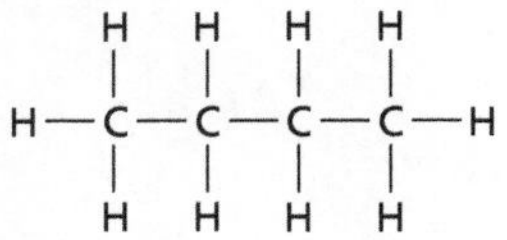

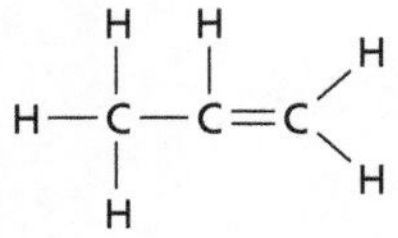

(A) I only Ⓐ

(B) I and III only Ⓑ

(C) II and III only Ⓒ

(D) I, II and III Ⓓ

Items <u>8–9</u> refer to the following reaction between propene and Y.

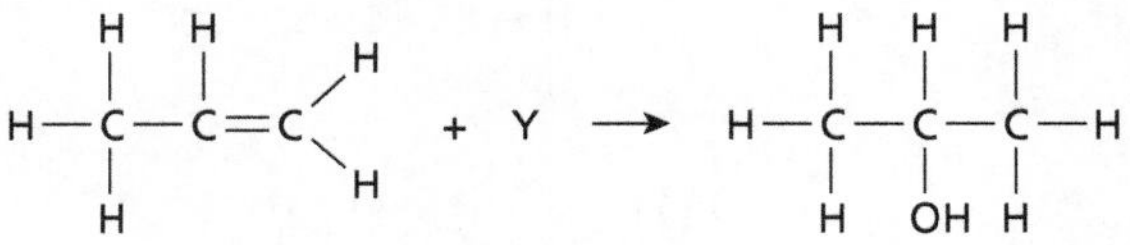

8 What is the MOST likely identity of Y?

(A) Water Ⓐ

(B) Steam Ⓑ

(C) Acidified potassium manganate(VII) Ⓒ

(D) Acidified hydrogen peroxide Ⓓ

9 Which of the following is NOT required for the reaction?

(A) A temperature of about 300 °C Ⓐ

(B) Phosphoric acid in sand Ⓑ

(C) A pressure of about 70 atm Ⓒ

(D) Concentrated sulfuric acid Ⓓ

10 Which would be the BEST test to distinguish between butane and butene?

(A) Burn them both in a plentiful supply of oxygen   Ⓐ

(B) React them both with chlorine gas   Ⓑ

(C) React them both with bromine solution   Ⓒ

(D) React them both with hydrogen bromide gas   Ⓓ

11 Natural gas is regarded as a good fuel because

    I it has a high heat of combustion

    II it is a fossil fuel

    III it burns with a clean, blue flame

(A) II only   Ⓐ

(B) I and III only   Ⓑ

(C) II and III only   Ⓒ

(D) I, II and III   Ⓓ

12 Which of the following statements about biogas is INCORRECT?

(A) Biogas is a non-renewable energy source.   Ⓐ

(B) Biogas can be used as a fuel for cooking.   Ⓑ

(C) The main component of biogas is methane.   Ⓒ

(D) Biogas can be produced from waste organic matter.   Ⓓ

13 Which of the following statements about alcohols is true?

(A) Their molecules are non-polar.   Ⓐ

(B) They are less volatile than their corresponding alkanes.   Ⓑ

(C) They are insoluble in water.   Ⓒ

(D) The smallest alcohols are gases at room temperature.   Ⓓ

Items **14–15** refer to the reaction scheme below.

$$Q \xleftarrow[\text{170°C}]{\text{Conc } H_2SO_4} CH_3CH_2OH \xrightarrow[\text{Heat}]{+ H^+/K_2Cr_2O_7} R \xrightarrow{+ Ca} S + H_2(g)$$

$$\downarrow + Na$$

$$T + H_2(g)$$

14 The MOST accurate structural formula of T is:

(A)

$$H-\overset{\overset{\displaystyle H}{|}}{\underset{\underset{\displaystyle H}{|}}{C}}-\overset{\overset{\displaystyle H}{|}}{\underset{\underset{\displaystyle H}{|}}{C}}-O-Na$$

(B)

$$H-\overset{\overset{\displaystyle H}{|}}{\underset{\underset{\displaystyle H}{|}}{C}}-C\overset{\displaystyle O}{\underset{\displaystyle O-Na}{<}}$$

(C)

$$H-\overset{\overset{\displaystyle H}{|}}{\underset{\underset{\displaystyle H}{|}}{C}}-\overset{\overset{\displaystyle H}{|}}{\underset{\underset{\displaystyle H}{|}}{C}}-O^-Na^+$$

(D)

$$H-\overset{\overset{\displaystyle H}{|}}{\underset{\underset{\displaystyle H}{|}}{C}}-C\overset{\displaystyle O}{\underset{\displaystyle O^-Na^+}{<}}$$

Ⓐ Ⓑ Ⓒ Ⓓ

15 Which compound is unsaturated?

(A) Q

(B) R

(C) S

(D) T

Ⓐ Ⓑ Ⓒ Ⓓ

16 The breathalyser test detects the presence of ethanol in a driver's breath because the ethanol

(A) reduces the orange $Cr_2O_7^{2-}$ ion to the green Cr^{3+} ion

(B) oxidises the orange $Cr_2O_7^{2-}$ ion to the green Cr^{3+} ion

(C) reduces the green Cr^{3+} ion to the orange $Cr_2O_7^{2-}$ ion

(D) oxidises the green Cr^{3+} ion to the orange $Cr_2O_7^{2-}$ ion

Ⓐ Ⓑ Ⓒ Ⓓ

Items **17–19** refer to the following apparatus, which can be used to prepare a sample of ethanol in the laboratory.

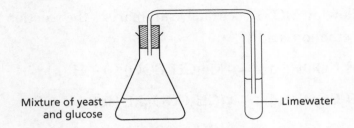

Mixture of yeast and glucose — Limewater

17 What reaction is occurring in the conical flask?

(A) Dehydration   Ⓐ

(B) Oxidation   Ⓑ

(C) Aerobic respiration   Ⓒ

(D) Fermentation   Ⓓ

18 A student set up the apparatus and left it for a week. What method could he use to obtain an almost pure sample of ethanol from the mixture in the flask?

(A) Evaporation   Ⓐ

(B) Simple distillation   Ⓑ

(C) Fractional distillation   Ⓒ

(D) Filtration   Ⓓ

19 Another student set up the apparatus and left it for several weeks and found that the pH of the mixture in the flask had decreased to 5. The BEST explanation for her observation is

(A) the yeast had used up all the glucose and had started to digest the ethanol into ethanoic acid   Ⓐ

(B) aerobic bacteria had entered the mixture and had started to oxidise the ethanol to ethanoic acid   Ⓑ

(C) the yeast cells had died and their decomposition had turned the mixture acidic   Ⓒ

(D) anaerobic bacteria had entered the mixture and converted any remaining glucose to ethanoic acid   Ⓓ

20 Which of the following MOST accurately summarises the reaction between magnesium and ethanoic acid?

(A) $Mg(s) + 2CH_3COOH(aq) \longrightarrow Mg(CH_3COO)_2(s) + H_2(g)$ Ⓐ

(B) $Mg(s) + 2CH_3COOH(aq) \longrightarrow (CH_3COO)_2Mg(aq) + H_2O(l)$ Ⓑ

(C) $Mg(s) + 2CH_3COOH(aq) \longrightarrow (CH_3COOH)_2Mg(aq) + H_2(g)$ Ⓒ

(D) $Mg(s) + 2CH_3COOH(aq) \longrightarrow (CH_3COO)_2Mg(aq) + H_2(g)$ Ⓓ

B4 Reactions of Carbon Compounds (2)

1 The reaction between ethanoic acid and ethanol is known as

    I a condensation reaction

    II an esterification reaction

    III an addition reaction

(A) III only Ⓐ

(B) I and II only Ⓑ

(C) II and III only Ⓒ

(D) I, II and III Ⓓ

2 Which of the following is NOT a reason for adding concentrated sulfuric acid to the reaction mixture when making an ester?

(A) To increase the yield of ester Ⓐ

(B) To speed up the reaction Ⓑ

(C) To remove any water produced Ⓒ

(D) To bring about the reaction Ⓓ

3 What is the name of the following compound?

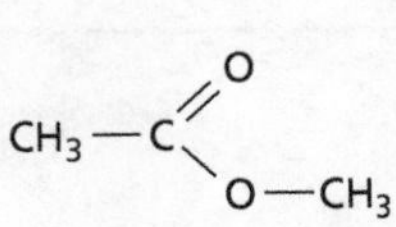

$$CH_3-C\underset{O-CH_3}{\overset{O}{\diagup}}$$

(A) Ethyl methanoate   Ⓐ

(B) Ethyl ethanoate   Ⓑ

(C) Methyl methanoate   Ⓒ

(D) Methyl ethanoate   Ⓓ

4 The formula of the compound formed by reacting propanoic acid and ethanol is

(A) $CH_3COOC_3H_7$ Ⓐ

(B) $C_2H_5COOC_2H_5$ Ⓑ

(C) $C_3H_7COOC_2H_5$ Ⓒ

(D) $C_3H_7COOC_3H_7$ Ⓓ

5 Acid hydrolysis of methyl butanoate forms

(A) methanoic acid and butanol   Ⓐ

(B) butanoic acid and water   Ⓑ

(C) butanoic acid and methanol   Ⓒ

(D) methanoic acid, butanol and water   Ⓓ

Item **6** refers to the following ester.

$$H-\overset{\overset{\displaystyle H}{|}}{\underset{\underset{\displaystyle H}{|}}{C}}-\overset{\overset{\displaystyle O}{\|}}{C}-O-\overset{\overset{\displaystyle H}{|}}{\underset{\underset{\displaystyle H}{|}}{C}}-\overset{\overset{\displaystyle H}{|}}{\underset{\underset{\displaystyle H}{|}}{C}}-\overset{\overset{\displaystyle H}{|}}{\underset{\underset{\displaystyle H}{|}}{C}}-H$$

6 Alkaline hydrolysis of the ester using sodium hydroxide solution would form

(A)

(B)

(C)

(D)

7 The MOST suitable name for the process by which soap is made from natural fats and oils is

(A) saponification

(B) esterification

(C) hydrolysis

(D) dehydration

8 Which statement is true about a soapless detergent but is untrue about a soapy detergent?

(A) The detergent removes greasy dirt from clothes.

(B) A lather is formed when the detergent is shaken with distilled water.

(C) The detergent does not form a precipitate in hard water.

(D) The detergent is made from natural fats and oils.

9 Which of the following correctly summarises addition and condensation polymerisation?

	Addition polymerisation	Condensation polymerisation
(A)	Only one product is produced	The empirical formulae of the polymer and monomer are the same
(B)	Only one type of monomer is usually used to make the polymer	Only one product is produced
(C)	Two products are produced	More than one type of monomer is usually used to make the polymer
(D)	The empirical formulae of the polymer and monomer are the same	Two products are produced

Ⓐ Ⓑ Ⓒ Ⓓ

10 Which of the following represents condensation polymerisation?

(A) $n(CH_2{=}CH_2) \longrightarrow (CH_2CH_2)_n$

(B) $XCOOH + YOH \longrightarrow XCOOY + H_2O$

(C) $nOH{-}Z{-}OH \longrightarrow (O{-}Z)_n + nH_2O$

(D) $6CO_2 + 6H_2O \longrightarrow C_6H_{12}O_6 + 6O_2$

Ⓐ Ⓑ Ⓒ Ⓓ

11 The polymer PVC can be represented by the following structure.

$$-CHCl{-}CH_2{-}CHCl{-}CH_2{-}CHCl{-}CH_2{-}$$

The monomer of PVC would be

(A) $CH_2Cl{-}CH_3$

(B) $CHCl{=}CH_2$

(C) $CHCl{=}CH_3$

(D) $CH_2{=}CH_3$

Ⓐ Ⓑ Ⓒ Ⓓ

Items **12–13** refer to the following compounds.

I

H—O—C—C—O—H

II

H—C—C=C—C—H

III

C—C—C

H—O   O—H

IV

C=C—C

H   O—H

12 Which TWO compounds will undergo condensation polymerisation?

(A) I and III

(B) I and IV

(C) II and III

(D) II and IV

(A)
(B)
(C)
(D)

13 Which compound(s) is/are capable of undergoing addition polymerisation?

(A) II only

(B) I and III only

(C) II and IV only

(D) I, III and IV only

(A)
(B)
(C)
(D)

Item **14** refers to the following partial structure of a polymer.

—N—☐—N—C—☐—C—N—☐—N—C—☐—C—

14 Which monomers were used to make the polymer?

(A) 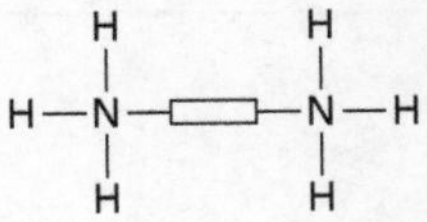 and

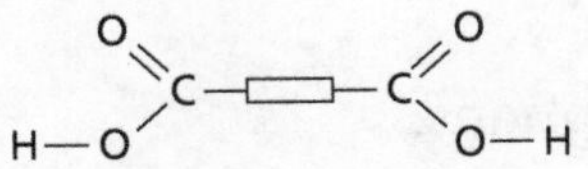

(B) 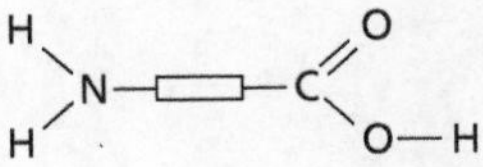 and

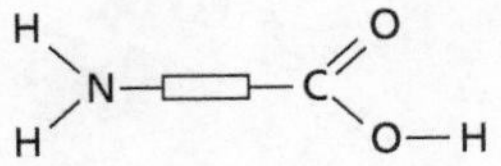

(C) 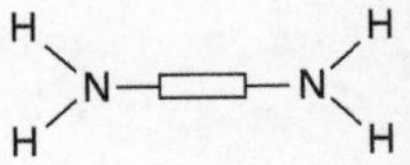 and

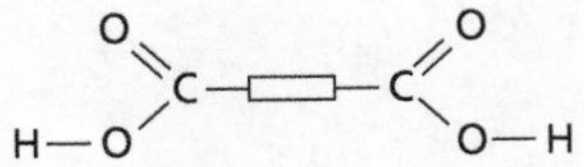

(D) 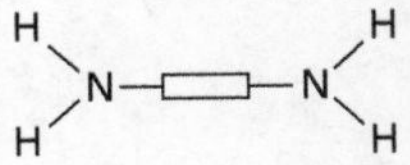 and

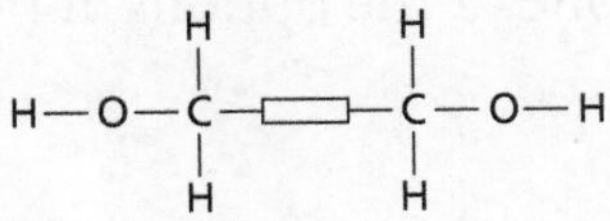

$$\text{(A)} \quad \text{(B)} \quad \text{(C)} \quad \text{(D)}$$

Item 15 refers to the structure of the artificial sweetener, aspartame, shown below.

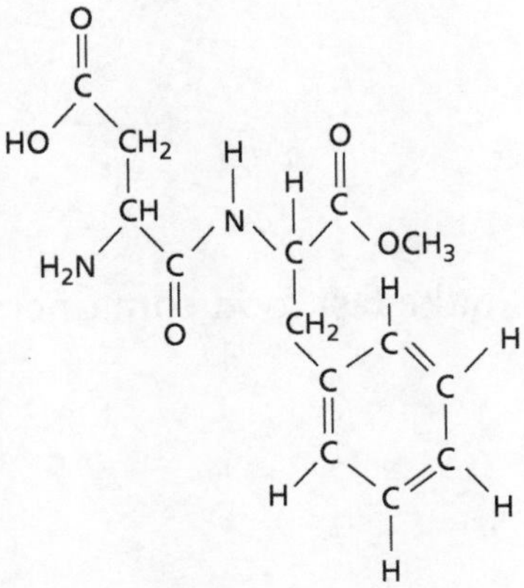

15 Which of the following are present in aspartame?

    I The hydroxyl functional group

    II An ester linkage

    III An amide linkage

(A) I and II only

(B) I and III only

(C) II and III only

(D) I, II and III

Items **16–17** refer to the following options.

(A) Protein

(B) Nylon

(C) Terylene

(D) Polystyrene

Match EACH item below with one of the options above. Each option may be used once, more than once or not at all.

16 Is a synthetic polyamide?

(A)   Ⓐ

(B)   Ⓑ

(C)   Ⓒ

(D)   Ⓓ

17 Is MOST likely to be used to make fast food containers?

(A)   Ⓐ

(B)   Ⓑ

(C)   Ⓒ

(D)   Ⓓ

18 Which of the following INCORRECTLY matches the polymer with its use?

	Polymer	Use	
(A)	Polypropene	To make items of clothing that stretch	Ⓐ
(B)	Polychloroethene (PVC)	To make guttering	Ⓑ
(C)	Starch	Stored as a food reserve in plants	Ⓒ
(D)	Polyethene	To make plastic bags	Ⓓ

Section C: Inorganic Chemistry
C1 Characteristics of Metals

1 All metals

    I lose electrons when they ionise

    II react with oxygen in the air

    III are solid at room temperature

(A) I only   (A)

(B) I and II only   (B)

(C) II and III only   (C)

(D) I, II and III   (D)

2 Metals are malleable because

(A) the cations in the lattice are mobile   (A)

(B) the lattice contains delocalised electrons which can move   (B)

(C) the atoms in the lattice can roll over each other when pressure is applied   (C)

(D) the atoms in the lattice are different sizes so can slide past each other easily   (D)

3 When metals react they

(A) remove electrons from the other reactant   (A)

(B) cause an increase in oxidation number of another reactant   (B)

(C) can form both ionic and covalent bonds with the other reactant   (C)

(D) behave as reducing agents   (D)

4 Metal W reacts fairly vigorously with dilute sulfuric acid, burns easily and reacts very slowly with cold water. The MOST likely identity of W is

(A) sodium   (A)

(B) copper   (B)

(C) iron   (C)

(D) magnesium   (D)

5 Zinc atoms can be converted to Zn^{2+} ions by

    I adding the zinc to hydrochloric acid

    II heating the zinc in air

    III adding the zinc to cold water

(A) I only   Ⓐ

(B) I and II only   Ⓑ

(C) II and III only   Ⓒ

(D) I, II and III   Ⓓ

6 When a metal reacts with cold water it forms

(A) a hydroxide   Ⓐ

(B) an oxide   Ⓑ

(C) a salt   Ⓒ

(D) oxygen   Ⓓ

7 Which of the following would produce hydrogen?

    I Copper and sulfuric acid

    II Aluminium and steam

    III Sodium and water

(A) I only   Ⓐ

(B) III only   Ⓑ

(C) II and III only   Ⓒ

(D) I, II and III   Ⓓ

8 The following equations correctly summarise the reactions of metals and their compounds EXCEPT

(A) $CaO(s) + 2HNO_3(aq) \longrightarrow Ca(NO_3)_2(aq) + H_2O(l)$ Ⓐ

(B) $Cu(s) + 2HCl(aq) \longrightarrow CuCl_2(aq) + H_2(g)$ Ⓑ

(C) $ZnCO_3(s) + H_2SO_4(aq) \longrightarrow ZnSO_4(aq) + CO_2(g) + H_2O(l)$ Ⓒ

(D) $Mg(OH)_2(s) + 2HCl(aq) \longrightarrow MgCl_2(aq) + 2H_2O(l)$ Ⓓ

9 Metal X forms an oxide that reacts with acids but not with strong alkalis.

Metal Y forms an oxide that reacts with acids and strong alkalis.

Metal Z forms a hydroxide that is not decomposed by heating.

Which combination BEST identifies X, Y and Z?

	X	Y	Z	
(A)	Calcium	Zinc	Magnesium	Ⓐ
(B)	Iron	Aluminium	Sodium	Ⓑ
(C)	Aluminium	Sodium	Calcium	Ⓒ
(D)	Magnesium	Copper	Potassium	Ⓓ

10 Which of the following statements are true of all nitrates when they are heated?

I Brown fumes are produced.

II There is a colour change.

III Oxygen is evolved.

IV There is a decrease in mass.

(A) I and II only   Ⓐ

(B) II and III only   Ⓑ

(C) III and IV only   Ⓒ

(D) I, III and IV only   Ⓓ

11 Which of the following equations is INCORRECT?

(A) $CaCO_3(s) \xrightarrow{heat} CaO(s) + CO_2(g)$ Ⓐ

(B) $Al_2(CO_3)_3(s) \xrightarrow{heat} Al_2O_3(s) + 3CO_2(g)$ Ⓑ

(C) $CuCO_3(s) \xrightarrow{heat} CuO(s) + CO_2(g)$ Ⓒ

(D) $Na_2CO_3(s) \xrightarrow{heat} Na_2O(s) + CO_2(g)$ Ⓓ

C2 Reactivity and Extraction of Metals

1 Which of the following is NOT used as a basis for arranging metals in the reactivity series?

(A) How vigorously they react with dilute acids   (A)

(B) How vigorously they react with each other   (B)

(C) How easily their compounds are decomposed when heated   (C)

(D) How easily they displace each other from their compounds   (D)

2 Metal X burns vigorously when heated in air, whereas metal Y burns only when heated very strongly. Which of the following is the correct descending order of reactivity of metal X, metal Y, copper and magnesium?

(A) Magnesium, metal X, metal Y, copper   (A)

(B) Metal X, magnesium, copper, metal Y   (B)

(C) Copper, metal Y, metal X, magnesium   (C)

(D) Metal X, magnesium, metal Y, copper   (D)

3 Which of the following is/are correct?

    I When heated, potassium nitrate does not decompose, but copper(II) nitrate decomposes readily.

    II Calcium hydroxide decomposes when heated to form calcium oxide and steam.

    III Magnesium carbonate decomposes more readily than zinc carbonate when both are heated.

(A) II only   (A)

(B) I and II only   (B)

(C) I and III only   (C)

(D) I, II and III   (D)

4 The following data refer to four metals, R, S, T and U.

Metal	Reacts with dilute hydrochloric acid	Occurs in nature as compounds
R	✗	✓
S	✗	✗
T	✓	✓
U	✓	✓

✓ = yes
✗ = no

When U is added to an aqueous solution of a salt of T, a precipitate forms.

The correct order of these metals in the reactivity series is:

(A) T, U, R, S Ⓐ

(B) T, U, S, R Ⓑ

(C) U, T, R, S Ⓒ

(D) U, T, S, R Ⓓ

Item 5 refers to the following experiment, which was set up and observed periodically for 1 hour:

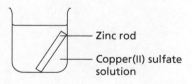

5 After 1 hour the following observations were made EXCEPT

(A) The solution had become paler blue Ⓐ

(B) The zinc rod had decreased in size Ⓑ

(C) The volume of the solution had decreased Ⓒ

(D) Pink particles had collected at the bottom of the beaker Ⓓ

<u>Item 6</u> refers to the following investigation, which was set up and left for 3 hours.

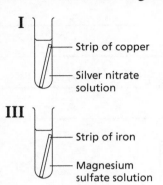

II

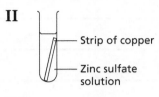

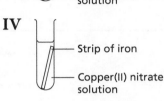

6. At the end of the investigation, metal was deposited in

(A) tubes I and III

(B) tubes I and IV

(C) tubes II and III

(D) tubes II and IV

7. Which of the following is found in the Earth's crust in its elemental state?

(A) Silver

(B) Iron

(C) Calcium

(D) Zinc

8. The method used to extract a metal from its ore depends on the

(A) reactivity of the ore

(B) position of the ore in the reactivity series

(C) melting point of the ore

(D) position of the metal in the reactivity series

9 The process by which any metal is extracted from its ore is

(A) reduction   Ⓐ

(B) electrolysis   Ⓑ

(C) displacement   Ⓒ

(D) decomposition   Ⓓ

10 For reference, carbon can be placed between aluminium and zinc in the reactivity series of metals. Which metals could be extracted from their ores by reacting with carbon?

     I Copper

     II Iron

     III Magnesium

(A) I only   Ⓐ

(B) III only   Ⓑ

(C) I and II only   Ⓒ

(D) I, II and III   Ⓓ

11 To extract aluminium from alumina, the alumina is dissolved in molten cryolite to

     I reduce its melting point

     II improve its electrical conductivity

     III separate its ions

(A) I only   Ⓐ

(B) I and II only   Ⓑ

(C) II and III only   Ⓒ

(D) I, II and III   Ⓓ

Item 12 refers to the following electrolytic cell, which is used to extract aluminium from its ore.

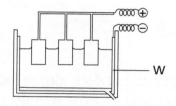

12 Which equation correctly summarises the reaction occurring at W?

(A) $Al^{3+}(l) + 3e^- \longrightarrow Al(l)$

(B) $Al^{3+}(l) \longrightarrow Al(l) + 3e^-$

(C) $2O^{2-}(l) \longrightarrow O_2(g) + 4e^-$

(D) $2O^{2-}(l) + 4e^- \longrightarrow O_2(g)$

Ⓐ
Ⓑ
Ⓒ
Ⓓ

13 Which is NOT a raw material used in the extraction of iron?

(A) Carbon monoxide

(B) Limestone

(C) Air

(D) Haematite

Ⓐ
Ⓑ
Ⓒ
Ⓓ

Items **14–15** refer to the blast furnace illustrated below.

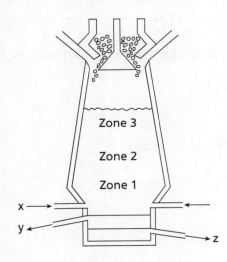

14 The correct equation for the reaction occurring in Zone 1 is

(A) $CO_2(g) + C(s) \longrightarrow 2CO(g)$

(B) $2C(s) + O_2(g) \longrightarrow 2CO(g)$

(C) $C(s) + O_2(g) \longrightarrow CO_2(g)$

(D) $Fe_2O_3(s) + 3CO(g) \longrightarrow 2Fe(l) + 3CO_2(g)$

Ⓐ

Ⓑ

Ⓒ

Ⓓ

15 Which of the following correctly identifies X, Y and Z?

	X	Y	Z	
(A)	Hot carbon dioxide	Molten iron	Molten calcium silicate	Ⓐ
(B)	Hot air	Molten calcium silicate	Molten iron	Ⓑ
(C)	Hot air	Molten iron	Molten calcium silicate	Ⓒ
(D)	Hot carbon dioxide	Molten calcium silicate	Molten iron	Ⓓ

16 Limestone is added to a blast furnace to

(A) produce carbon dioxide

(B) produce carbon monoxide

(C) remove slag from the iron ore

(D) remove silicon dioxide from the iron ore

C3 Uses of Metals

1 Wrought iron can be used to make ornamental ironwork because it is

    I malleable and ductile

    II easily welded

    III extremely resistant to corrosion

(A) III only   Ⓐ

(B) I and II only   Ⓑ

(C) II and III only   Ⓒ

(D) I, II and III   Ⓓ

2 Which of the following is NOT a reason for using aluminium to make cans to store drinks?

(A) Aluminium is resistant to corrosion   Ⓐ

(B) Aluminium is non-toxic   Ⓑ

(C) Aluminium is a good conductor of heat   Ⓒ

(D) Aluminium is malleable   Ⓓ

3 Which of the following is the BEST reason for using lead as a radiation shield?

(A) Lead is very malleable   Ⓐ

(B) Lead has a high density   Ⓑ

(C) Lead conducts electricity   Ⓒ

(D) Lead is resistant to corrosion   Ⓓ

4 Saucepans can be made out of aluminium because

(A) aluminium is coated with an unreactive layer of aluminium oxide   Ⓐ

(B) aluminium is a good insulator   Ⓑ

(C) aluminium is an unreactive metal   Ⓒ

(D) aluminium has a high density   Ⓓ

5 Metals are often alloyed with other metals

    I to make them stronger

    II to make them more resistant to corrosion

    III to increase their electrical conductivity

(A) I only   Ⓐ

(B) III only   Ⓑ

(C) I and II only   Ⓒ

(D) I, II and III   Ⓓ

6 Which of the following statements is/are correct?

    I Magnalium is an alloy of aluminium and copper.

    II Lead solder is an alloy of lead and tin.

    III Cast iron contains a lower percentage of carbon than high carbon steel.

(A) I only   Ⓐ

(B) II only   Ⓑ

(C) II and III only   Ⓒ

(D) I, II and III   Ⓓ

Items **7–9** refer to the following options.

(A) Lead solder

(B) High carbon steel

(C) Stainless steel

(D) Duralumin

Match EACH item below with one of the options above. Each option may be used once, more than once or not at all.

7 Is used to construct aircraft?

(A)   Ⓐ

(B)   Ⓑ

(C)   Ⓒ

(D)   Ⓓ

8 Has a very shiny attractive appearance?

(A)   Ⓐ

(B)   Ⓑ

(C)   Ⓒ

(D)   Ⓓ

9 Is used to join metal items together?

(A)   Ⓐ

(B)   Ⓑ

(C)   Ⓒ

(D)   Ⓓ

10 Which of the following is used MOST widely in the construction industry?

(A) Cast iron   Ⓐ

(B) High carbon steel   Ⓑ

(C) Stainless steel   Ⓒ

(D) Mild steel   Ⓓ

C4 Impact of Metals on Living Systems and the Environment

1 An experiment was set up to investigate the conditions necessary for rusting. In which tube would the iron nail rust the fastest?

(A)  Tap water   Ⓐ

(B) 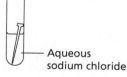 Aqueous sodium chloride   Ⓑ

                                                                       Ⓒ

(C) Oil / Boiled and cooled tap water   Ⓓ

(D) Calcium chloride

2 Which of the following statements is correct?

(A) The corrosion of iron is beneficial because hydrated iron(III) oxide has an attractive orange appearance. Ⓐ

(B) The corrosion of iron and aluminium is known as rusting. Ⓑ

(C) The corrosion of aluminium is beneficial because it forms a layer of aluminium hydroxide that protects the surface of the aluminium. Ⓒ

(D) The corrosion of iron is detrimental because hydrated iron(III) oxide readily flakes off. Ⓓ

<u>Items 3–5</u> refer to the following options.

(A) Magnesium

(B) Calcium

(C) Iron

(D) Carbon

Match EACH item below with one of the options above. Each option may be used once, more than once or not at all.

3 Is necessary to produce haemoglobin?

(A) Ⓐ

(B) Ⓑ

(C) Ⓒ

(D) Ⓓ

4 Helps to prevent rickets?

(A) Ⓐ

(B) Ⓑ

(C) Ⓒ

(D) Ⓓ

5 Forms part of the chlorophyll molecule?

(A) Ⓐ

(B) Ⓑ

(C) Ⓒ

(D) Ⓓ

6 Which of the following is classified as a trace element required by living organisms?

(A) Potassium Ⓐ

(B) Zinc Ⓑ

(C) Lead Ⓒ

(D) Calcium Ⓓ

7 One of the major sources of cadmium in the environment is

(A) smoke from bush fires Ⓐ

(B) volcanic eruptions Ⓑ

(C) discarded car batteries Ⓒ

(D) cigarette smoke Ⓓ

8 The concentration of mercury in the body tissues of organisms in an aquatic environment is given in the table below.

Organism	Mercury concentration/parts per million
Shrimp	0.035
Rooted aquatic plants	nil
Mackerel	0.237
Planktonic plants	0.002
Marlin	0.448

The MOST likely food chain is

(A) Rooted aquatic plants ⟶ shrimp ⟶ mackerel ⟶ marlin   Ⓐ

(B) Planktonic plants ⟶ mackerel ⟶ shrimp ⟶ marlin   Ⓑ

(C) Planktonic plants ⟶ shrimp ⟶ mackerel ⟶ marlin   Ⓒ

(D) Rooted aquatic plants ⟶ shrimp ⟶ marlin ⟶ mackerel   Ⓓ

9 Which of the following statements in MOST likely to be INCORRECT?

(A) Inhalation of cadmium can lead to anaemia.   Ⓐ

(B) Lead is particularly harmful to young children.   Ⓑ

(C) Ingestion of arsenic can cause changes to the skin.   Ⓒ

(D) Minamata disease can be caused by ingesting methyl mercury.   Ⓓ

10 Which of the following would be the BEST way to solve the problem of the disposal of solid waste items containing heavy metals?

(A) Incinerate the items   Ⓐ

(B) Place the items in landfills   Ⓑ

(C) Recycle the items   Ⓒ

(D) Throw the items into the oceans   Ⓓ

C5 Non-metals (1)

1 All non-metals

    I gain electrons when they ionise

    II are poor conductors of electricity

    III react with reactive metals

(A) I only   Ⓐ

(B) II only   Ⓑ

(C) I and III only   Ⓒ

(D) I, II and III   Ⓓ

2 The following are gases at room temperature EXCEPT

(A) chlorine Ⓐ

(B) hydrogen Ⓑ

(C) sulfur Ⓒ

(D) nitrogen Ⓓ

3 When non-metals react with metals, the non-metal

(A) behaves as a reducing agent Ⓐ

(B) removes electrons from the metal atoms Ⓑ

(C) can form both ionic and covalent compounds Ⓒ

(D) causes the oxidation number of the metal to decrease Ⓓ

4 In which reactions is the non-metal behaving as an oxidising agent?

$\text{I } 2KI(aq) + Br_2(aq) \longrightarrow 2KBr(aq) + I_2(aq)$

$\text{II } CO_2(g) + C(s) \longrightarrow 2CO(g)$

$\text{III } 3Mg(s) + N_2(g) \longrightarrow Mg_3N_2(s)$

$\text{IV } PbO(s) + H_2(g) \longrightarrow Pb(s) + H_2O(g)$

(A) I and III only Ⓐ

(B) I and IV only Ⓑ

(C) II and III only Ⓒ

(D) II and IV only Ⓓ

5 Which list contains non-metals that can all behave as reducing agents?

(A) Sulfur, chlorine, hydrogen, nitrogen Ⓐ

(B) Carbon, sulfur, oxygen, hydrogen Ⓑ

(C) Nitrogen, carbon, chlorine, oxygen Ⓒ

(D) Hydrogen, sulfur, carbon, nitrogen Ⓓ

6 MOST oxides produced when non-metals react with oxygen are

(A) acidic (A)

(B) neutral (B)

(C) basic (C)

(D) amphoteric (D)

<u>Items 7–9</u> refer to the following apparatus used by a student to produce carbon dioxide in the laboratory.

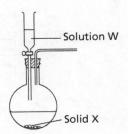

7 The MOST suitable identities of W and X would be:

	W	X	
(A)	Nitric acid	Magnesium carbonate	(A)
(B)	Sulfuric acid	Calcium carbonate	(B)
(C)	Glucose solution	Yeast	(C)
(D)	Hydrochloric acid	Lead(II) carbonate	(D)

8 Which drying agent(s) could be used to dry the gas after it is produced?

    I Concentrated sulfuric acid

    II Anhydrous calcium chloride

    III Calcium oxide

(A) I only (A)

(B) I and II only (B)

(C) II and III only (C)

(D) I, II and III (D)

9 Which apparatus would the student use to collect the gas after it was dried?

(A)

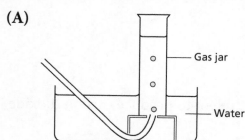

Gas jar

Water

(B)

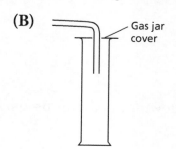

Gas jar cover

(C)

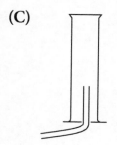

(D)

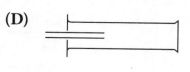

10 Which statement is correct?

(A) Ammonia can be prepared in the laboratory by reacting calcium oxide and ammonium chloride.

(B) The most suitable agent to dry ammonia is concentrated sulfuric acid.

(C) Dry ammonia can be collected by upward displacement of air.

(D) Wet ammonia can be collected by displacement of water.

11 Oxygen can be prepared in the laboratory by adding hydrogen peroxide to manganese(IV) oxide. The manganese(IV) oxide

(A) reacts with the hydrogen peroxide

(B) acts as a catalyst

(C) behaves as a reducing agent

(D) provides the source of oxygen

12 The following statements are correct EXCEPT

(A) Carbon dioxide is used to make carbonated soft drinks because it adds a pleasant tingle and taste ⓐ

(B) Oxygen is used in welding torches because it is essential for combustion Ⓑ

(C) Carbon dioxide is used in fire extinguishers because it is less dense than air Ⓒ

(D) Oxygen is used in hospitals to ease certain medical disorders because it is essential for respiration Ⓓ

C6 Non-metals (2)

Items **1–2** refer to the following options.

(A) Silicon

(B) Carbon

(C) Chlorine

(D) Sulfur

Match EACH item below with one of the options above. Each option may be used once, more than once or not at all.

1 Is used to harden the rubber in car tyres?

(A) ⓐ

(B) Ⓑ

(C) Ⓒ

(D) Ⓓ

2 Its compounds are used to make ceramics?

(A) ⓐ

(B) Ⓑ

(C) Ⓒ

(D) Ⓓ

3 Chlorine is used to make all of the following EXCEPT

(A) antiseptics Ⓐ

(B) antibiotics Ⓑ

(C) bleaching agents Ⓒ

(D) dry cleaning fluids Ⓓ

4 The compounds of which element would NOT be used to make fertilisers?

(A) Nitrogen Ⓐ

(B) Phosphorus Ⓑ

(C) Carbon Ⓒ

(D) Sulfur Ⓓ

5 Which of the following contribute(s) to the formation of acid rain?

    I Carbon monoxide

    II Sulfur dioxide

    III Nitrogen dioxide

(A) II only Ⓐ

(B) I and III only Ⓑ

(C) II and III only Ⓒ

(D) I, II and III Ⓓ

6 Which of the following is UNLIKELY to be a consequence of the build-up of carbon dioxide in the upper atmosphere that is being caused by human activities?

(A) Glaciers and polar ice caps melting Ⓐ

(B) Gradual breakdown of the ozone layer in the upper atmosphere Ⓑ

(C) Weather patterns becoming more severe Ⓒ

(D) Global temperatures increasing Ⓓ

7 Incomplete combustion of fossil fuels produces

(A) carbon monoxide   (A)

(B) carbon dioxide   (B)

(C) sulfur dioxide   (C)

(D) chlorofluorocarbons   (D)

8 The following statements are true EXCEPT

(A) Nitrates and phosphates can cause eutrophication.   (A)

(B) Pesticides often harm top consumers in a food chain.   (B)

(C) Chlorofluorocarbons are starting to cause ocean acidification.   (C)

(D) Hydrogen sulfide is very toxic.   (D)

9 Which of the following correctly match(es) each property of water with its consequence?

	Property	Consequence
I	Water has a high heat of vaporisation	Sweating is an efficient cooling mechanism
II	Water dissolves many substances	Water can become polluted
III	Water has relatively high melting and boiling points	At the temperatures experienced on Earth, most water is in the gaseous state

(A) II only   (A)

(B) I and II only   (B)

(C) I and III only   (C)

(D) I, II and III   (D)

Item **10** refers to the following illustration which shows a lake in winter.

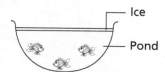

10 Which property of water is illustrated?

(A) Water has a relatively high melting point.

(B) Water has a high specific heat capacity.

(C) Water is not very volatile.

(D) Water has a maximum density at 4 °C.

Ⓐ

Ⓑ

Ⓒ

Ⓓ

11 Which of the following combinations is correct?

	Temporary water hardness	Permanent water hardness
(A)	Caused by dissolved calcium hydrogencarbonate	Can be removed by boiling
(B)	Caused by dissolved calcium sulfate	Cannot be removed by boiling
(C)	Can be removed by boiling	Caused by dissolved calcium sulfate
(D)	Cannot be removed by boiling	Caused by dissolved calcium hydrogencarbonate

Ⓐ

Ⓑ

Ⓒ

Ⓓ

12 Which list gives methods that can be used to treat water in the home?

(A) Filtering, softening, boiling, chlorinating

(B) Boiling, flocculating, filtering, softening

(C) Chlorinating, boiling, flocculating, filtering

(D) Softening, flocculating, chlorinating, filtering

Ⓐ

Ⓑ

Ⓒ

Ⓓ

13 Which equation MOST accurately shows how hard water can be softened?

(A) $Ca(HCO_3)_2(aq) \xrightarrow{heat} CaCO_3(aq) + H_2O(l) + CO_2(g)$

(B) $CaSO_4(aq) + Na_2CO_3(aq) \longrightarrow CaCO_3(aq) + Na_2SO_4(aq)$

(C) $Ca^{2+}(aq) + 2NaZ(s) \longrightarrow CaZ_2(s) + 2Na^+(aq)$

(D) $Ca^{2+}(aq) + CO_3^{2-}(aq) \longrightarrow CaCO_3(s)$

Ⓐ

Ⓑ

Ⓒ

Ⓓ

14 Which is NOT a benefit of Green Chemistry?

(A) Reduced pollution   Ⓐ

(B) Reduced energy usage   Ⓑ

(C) Reduced wastage   Ⓒ

(D) Reduced competitiveness of chemical manufacturers   Ⓓ

15 The principles of Green Chemistry include

     I carrying out processes at room temperature and pressure

     II using non-renewable feedstocks

     III designing products which persist in the environment when discarded

     IV preventing waste from being produced

(A) I and III only   Ⓐ

(B) I and IV only   Ⓑ

(C) I, II and IV only   Ⓒ

(D) II, III and IV only   Ⓓ

C7 Qualitative Analysis

Item 1 refers to the reaction scheme given below.

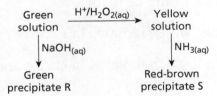

1 Which of the following correctly summarises the formation of precipitates R and S?

	R	S	
(A)	$Cu^{2+}(aq) + 2OH^{-}(aq) \longrightarrow Cu(OH)_2(s)$	$Fe^{3+}(aq) + 3OH^{-}(aq) \longrightarrow Fe(OH)_3(s)$	Ⓐ
(B)	$Fe^{3+}(aq) + 3OH^{-}(aq) \longrightarrow Fe(OH)_3(s)$	$Fe^{2+}(aq) + 2OH^{-}(aq) \longrightarrow Fe(OH)_2(s)$	Ⓑ
(C)	$Cu^{2+}(aq) + 2OH^{-}(aq) \longrightarrow Cu(OH)_2(s)$	$Fe^{2+}(aq) + 2OH^{-}(aq) \longrightarrow Fe(OH)_2(s)$	Ⓒ
(D)	$Fe^{2+}(aq) + 2OH^{-}(aq) \longrightarrow Fe(OH)_2(s)$	$Fe^{3+}(aq) + 3OH^{-}(aq) \longrightarrow Fe(OH)_3(s)$	Ⓓ

2 A student added sodium hydroxide solution to two solutions, P and Q, until in excess and determined the height of the precipitate at regular intervals.

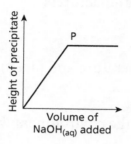

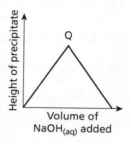

Which of the following gives the MOST likely identities of solutions P and Q?

	P	Q	
(A)	Calcium nitrate	Aluminium nitrate	Ⓐ
(B)	Zinc nitrate	Lead(II) nitrate	Ⓑ
(C)	Copper(II) nitrate	Calcium nitrate	Ⓒ
(D)	Aluminium nitrate	Iron(II) nitrate	Ⓓ

3 Aqueous ammonia is added, until in excess, to a solution containing Cu^{2+} ions. Which of the following observations would be made?

(A) A blue precipitate forms, which remains in excess. Ⓐ

(B) A blue precipitate forms, which remains in excess and turns deep blue on standing. Ⓑ

(C) A blue precipitate forms, which dissolves in excess forming a deep blue solution. Ⓒ

(D) No precipitate forms and the solution remains pale blue. Ⓓ

Items **4–5** refer to the following table.

	Effect of excess aqueous sodium hydroxide	Effect of excess aqueous ammonia	Effect of aqueous potassium iodide
(A)	No precipitate	No precipitate	No precipitate
(B)	No precipitate	White precipitate	Yellow precipitate
(C)	No precipitate	White precipitate	No precipitate
(D)	White precipitate	No precipitate	No precipitate

Match EACH ion below with one of the options in the table. Each option may be used once, more than once or not at all.

4 The Al^{3+} ion?

(A)

(B)

(C)

(D)

Ⓐ

Ⓑ

Ⓒ

Ⓓ

5 The Ca^{2+} ion?

(A)

(B)

(C)

(D)

Ⓐ

Ⓑ

Ⓒ

Ⓓ

6 A few drops of sodium hydroxide solution were added to an unknown ionic compound Z and no precipitate was seen. On warming, a pungent gas was evolved. The gas would MOST likely

   I turn red litmus paper blue

   II form dense white fumes with hydrogen chloride gas

   III turn acidified potassium dichromate(VI) solution from orange to green

(A) I only

(B) III only

(C) I and II only

(D) I, II and III

Ⓐ

Ⓑ

Ⓒ

Ⓓ

111

Item 7 refers to the following reaction scheme:

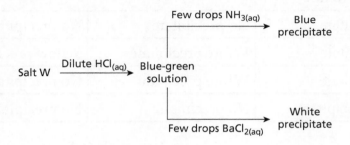

7 Salt W is

(A) copper(II) carbonate Ⓐ

(B) copper(II) sulfate Ⓑ

(C) iron(II) carbonate Ⓒ

(D) iron(II) sulfate Ⓓ

8 A few drops of silver nitrate solution were added to sodium chloride solution, followed by aqueous ammonia. Which of the following observations were made?

(A) A pale cream precipitate formed, which partially dissolved Ⓐ
in aqueous ammonia.

(B) A pale cream precipitate formed, which remained undissolved Ⓑ
in aqueous ammonia.

(C) A white precipitate formed, which partially dissolved in aqueous ammonia. Ⓒ

(D) A white precipitate formed, which dissolved in aqueous ammonia. Ⓓ

9 The following results were obtained when solids X and Y were heated separately in dry test tubes:

Solid X: a brown gas was produced and a glowing splint relit.

Solid Y: no gas was seen but a glowing splint relit.

The identities of X and Y are MOST likely to be

	X	Y	
(A)	Magnesium nitrate	Sodium nitrate	Ⓐ
(B)	Sodium bromide	Potassium nitrate	Ⓑ
(C)	Aluminium nitrate	Magnesium hydroxide	Ⓒ
(D)	Zinc nitrate	Calcium nitrate	Ⓓ

10 Which of the following test(s) could be used to distinguish between sodium bromide and sodium iodide?

   I Add hydrochloric acid to each and test the gas evolved

   II Add concentrated sulfuric acid to each, observe and test any gas evolved

   III Add silver nitrate solution to each and look at the colour of the precipitate

(A) I only   Ⓐ

(B) III only   Ⓑ

(C) II and III only   Ⓒ

(D) I, II and III   Ⓓ

Item **11** refers to the following experiment, which was set up to see if an unknown substance T contained the sulfite ion.

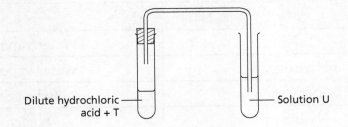

Dilute hydrochloric acid + T   Solution U

11 The MOST likely identity of solution U is

(A) acidified potassium manganate(VII) solution   Ⓐ

(B) lime water   Ⓑ

(C) acidified hydrogen peroxide   Ⓒ

(D) red litmus solution   Ⓓ

12 A few drops of concentrated sulfuric acid were added to solid V in a test tube and white fumes formed when a drop of concentrated ammonia solution was placed close to the tube. Solid V was MOST likely to be

(A) sodium chloride   Ⓐ

(B) sodium bromide   Ⓑ

(C) potassium carbonate.   Ⓒ

(D) potassium sulfite.   Ⓓ

13 Which of the following is responsible for the bleaching that occurs when chlorine comes into contact with moist blue litmus paper?

(A) Hydrochloric acid   Ⓐ

(B) The chlorate(I) ion   Ⓑ

(C) The chlorate(III) ion   Ⓒ

(D) The chloride ion   Ⓓ

14 A colourless, odourless gas, M, causes a burning splint to make a squeaky pop and, in doing so, forms another colourless, odourless gas, N, which causes dry cobalt(II) chloride paper to turn from blue to pink. Gases M and N are

	M	N	
(A)	Oxygen	Water vapour	Ⓐ
(B)	Hydrogen	Water vapour	Ⓑ
(C)	Water vapour	Hydrogen	Ⓒ
(D)	Hydrogen	Oxygen	Ⓓ

15 Which of the following correctly summarises the reaction occurring when carbon dioxide is bubbled into lime water?

(A) $Ca(OH)_2(aq) + 2CO_2(g) \longrightarrow Ca(HCO_3)_2(s)$ Ⓐ

(B) $CaO(aq) + CO_2(g) \longrightarrow CaCO_3(s)$ Ⓑ

(C) $CaCO_3(aq) + CO_2(g) + H_2O(l) \longrightarrow Ca(HCO_3)_2(s)$ Ⓒ

(D) $Ca(OH)_2(aq) + CO_2(g) \longrightarrow CaCO_3(s) + H_2O(l)$ Ⓓ